G000280532

THE UNIVERSE OF
SILVER BIRCH

THE UNIVERSE OF SILVER BIRCH

by

Frank Newman

Psychic Press Ltd,
2 Tavistock Chambers,
Bloomsbury Way,
London WC1A 2SE

First published in 1994

© Frank Newman

All rights reserved. No portion of this book may be reproduced or utilised in any form or by any means, electronic or mechanical, including photocopying, recording or retrieval system, without the prior permission in writing of the publisher. Nor is it to be otherwise circulated in any form or binding or cover other than that in which it is published.

ISBN 0 85384 088 1

Printed by Booksprint, West Street, St Philips, Bristol

CONTENTS

Foreword

THIS book outlines one man's pilgrimage towards a Truth which many seek in an effort to make sense of the world in which they find themselves.

It records the contribution that has been made in the search by the teachings of a spirit guide using the title of "Silver Birch," whose medium was Maurice Barbanell. I am no stranger to this guide, having been a member of his small circle for some 40-50 years, and I can pay homage to the importance of his teaching to a seeker after Truth.

He makes no claims to infallibility. He does not dogmatise, saying that the essence of dogma is to accept without reason. Silver Birch asks you test everything he says by the light of your own reason—if it measures up, accept it, if not, reject it. My own experience is that his words of wisdom make a direct appeal to the questing human heart.

Every person makes his own private pilgrimage. Mine started at the age of 22, when life seemed so obviously transient that I echoed the words of Studdert Kennedy, a first world war padre, who said, "No man can really be happy in this world until he is sure of the next."

At this stage, my mentor became the famous journalist, Hannen Swaffer who, with his friend Sir Edward Marshall Hall, had learned the truths of Spiritualism.

Jointly, they hired the old Queen's Hall to publicly testify to its truths. Under Swaffer's tutelage, I found this sometimes unpopular cause provided overwhelming evidence of survival.

Over the years, this has continued until, with humility, I can say with Ernest Oaten, late president of the International Spiritualist Federation, and the first person to broadcast these truths on National Radio on Friday, 13th April, 1934: "I assert that the evidence I have obtained makes it impossible for me to

4

doubt that I have talked with those who have passed through the gates of death. So strong is my conviction, that if I were the only man on earth who believed it, my faith would remain unshaken."

The present stage of the pilgrimage is to attempt to put into practice the truths learned over the years from Silver Birch. The most important of these being:

1. That this earthly life is a kindergarten of the spirit, where you learn lessons to equip you for the life to come.

2. To achieve a wider knowledge of the spiritual world — the real world — which is masked by materialism.

3. That God, or the Great Spirit, is the totality of all things. He is seen in the countless manifestations of natural phenomena. He is the epitome of law, love, wisdom and truth. He is the Infinite Intelligence operating ceaselessly in a mighty universe.

4. To achieve a wider understanding of prayer. To pray to the Great Spirit which is within and without, striving constantly through aspiration to establish a closer unity with that power.

Mr Newman's book makes its contribution to a wider knowledge of some of these great truths.

From experience, I have found that a great number of thoughtful and intelligent people, repelled by orthodox religion, are living in a kind of spiritual no man's land.

This was borne out some years ago, when Maurice Barbanell had a pitch at Speakers' Corner, Hyde Park, where he expounded the truths of the spirit.

On occasion, when he was on holiday or out of town, he would ask me to take his place. Spiritual matters were fair game for many of the crowd, who attended Speakers' Corner for the fun of things. I, however, found it very striking that, on descending from the rostrum, a good nucleus of people always remained behind. All expressed dissatisfaction with orthodox religion.

At a supplementary meeting I held in the park, though, they listened to, and were attracted by, the truths of the spirit. These people who are leaving, or have left, the church are those to whom these truths must be spread.

VERNON MOORE

5

The Silver Birch Books

Teachings of Silver Birch	first published in 1938
Guidance from Silver Birch	first published in 1966
Philosophy of Silver Birch	first published in 1969
More Philosophy of Silver Birch	first published in 1979
Light from Silver Birch	first published in 1983
Silver Birch Companion	first published in 1986
A Voice in the Wilderness	first published in 1986
The Seed of Truth	first published in 1987
The Spirit Speaks	first published in 1988
Lift up your Hearts	first published in 1990

The cassette, "Silver Birch Speaks", recorded at the Hannen Swaffer Home Circle, is available from the publishers Psychic Press Limited.

Acknowledgements

KNOWLEDGE is acquired during the course of one's life through the material processed through the mind and the manner in which it is interpreted by the individual. If we merely absorb the content of the material presented and do not analyse it, we do not extend the boundaries of our knowledge.

An open mind which is capable of analysing and making its own decisions through the application of common sense obtains far more satisfaction from life than the mind which has pre-set boundaries. An open mind functioning at an appropriate level of consciousness can also attract the interest of those who wish, unseen, to serve humanity.

The work of such authors as Dr Paul Brunton, Grace Cooke, Dr Walter J Kilner, Gris and Dick, Nandor Fodor, Janet and Colin Bord, Juan Mascaro, R.G. Medhurst, Muldoon and Carrington, W.E.R.Mons and Andrew Tomas, provided the catalysts, not unlike the pieces of a jig-saw puzzle, which in conjunction with regular periods of meditation, formulated my own view of the nature of the aura, or fields of energy, and the manner in which they relate to the universe.

This view, in my estimation, was completely endorsed by Professor H.S.Burr's work, which I chanced upon after reaching my own conclusions and the structure of the auric field presented by Vera Stanley Alder. Followed by the work of members of the International Institute of Biophysics, such as Dr Fritz Albert Popp, Dr Helmut Breithaup, Dr Walter Kroy, Dr Ulrich Warnke and Professor Herbert König which, wittingly or unwittingly, continued the work of Burr but without his perception, I am confident that through the processes gifted to me, my interpretation of the work of these persons of many talents is correct.

An introduction to the teachings of Silver Birch brought about the realisation that the scientific basis of the relationship of the auric or energy fields to the universe I had formulated contained the essential factors necessary at our level of perception to substantiate his words of wisdom. As the source of the teachings of Silver Birch stems from the Psychic Press, mainly through the compilations of Tony Ortzen, I must thank them, and the White Eagle Publishing Trust, for allowing me to quote so extensively from their publications in order to provide a touchstone for my analysis.

Knowledge for the benefit of humanity is, thankfully, not a commercial commodity and freely available to all who recognise its truths. Truth has many facets, but it is the level of conscious perception of the individual mind which selects the facet acceptable as truth.

Introduction

THE existence of the aura has been acknowledged by esoteric, psychic, spiritual and religious bodies, but, unfortunately, the structure and function of this phenomenon has not been established. This has been due, to a large extent, to the fact that although the sciences identify the auric field in terms of electromagnetic energy, they tend to ignore the esoteric connection.

The esoteric and religious groups have many interpretations of the structure of the auric field, but fail to grasp the implications of the truth central to their teachings, namely that "Spirit reigns supreme. It is the essence out of which all life is made for spirit is life and life is spirit." "It is the spirit that quickeneth, the flesh profiteth nothing — for the body without spirit is dead."

The essence of these teachings is that without Spirit, "out of which all life is made," there would be no physical manifestation in the manner we observe it today. "Spirit," therefore, is obviously the intelligence responsible for the development of all physical bodies.

The dictionary defines "Spirit" as "Any bodiless living being having intelligence and will" or "The element in man regarded as separable from and animating the body." The element "separable from and animating the body," as established in the course of out-of-body-experiences, is the astral body of the auric field. Therefore, it becomes acceptable that "all life" generated by Spirit functions through the auric field.

Scientific research into the auric field has been expressed in terms of "life," "bio," "electromagnetic fields" or "bioplasma," which, science would have us believe, is a

9

product of the physical body of matter. If, however, we accept that the intelligence for the maintenance and animation of the physical body lays within the auric field, "spirit," the process is reversed. Matter becomes a product of "spirit" and confirms the foregoing teachings.

Fortunately, slowly, but surely, there are a few members of the scientific fraternity who are gradually pushing aside these man-made barriers of prejudice to reveal much of that which has been termed the "mysteries." Therefore, if science wishes to establish the true nature of the universe it must take heed of religious and esoteric knowledge in order to give it direction.

Our mystics and seers, utilising the aura, can see, hear and describe those things that lie beyond the normal five senses of the vast majority. Problems arise when these sensitives are confronted by scientists of a sceptical nature. Sensitives can only debate their faculties in terms of what they see and hear, which, because of the lack of scientific data, the sceptic will not accept.

If the sensitives are to substantiate their claims in order to promote their philosophy — and at the same time provide an alternative view of life and the universe — they must have a scientific platform to support them. Without scientific data, it becomes almost impossible to promote any form of intellectual thought among those who, in one way or another, control the minds of the masses. The great exception to this statement is, of course, the well indoctrinated area of man-made religion. Through the advance of science, however, this situation is changing, but unfortunately the moral tone of society is declining. By directing their research in the right direction, science can rectify this matter by proving the true relationship of man to the universe.

During the course of my career in electrical engineering, I always felt there must be a scientific explanation of the so-called mysteries of the world in which we live. One cannot dismiss a variety of "mysterious" happenings, sometimes with many witnesses, as hallucinations, but throughout history, there have always been intellectuals who, for one reason or another, choose to dismiss these events out of hand. Because of their position in society, not that they are particularly versed in the subject to hand, their word is accepted as an authoritative statement on that particular subject. Authority can only be claimed if one spends sufficient time in diligent research into a particular field of interest, and then only at the level of comprehension of the individual. That level depends to a large extent on the integrity of the individual and his application.

Having spent a good proportion of my Government service in the tropics, witnessing many of the Hindu ceremonies such as fire walking and piercing the flesh with silver needles, spears and fish hooks without leaving any visible signs, it was only natural that on my retirement my mind would return to the "mysteries." With this interest as an incentive, I commenced reading scientific, philosophic and religious works, and over a period of approximately six years, sat in a variety of development circles. For one reason or the other, I found that progress in these circles was constantly thwarted, and eventually decided to commence meditation on my own on a regular basis.

Without the distraction of other sitters, I found it quite easy to meditate, and in a very short while reached a stage where I could empty my mind and enjoy a state of great peace and tranquillity interspersed with periods of great humility. Occasionally, while in this rather beautiful mental state, a sudden burst of inspiration would occur, either in picture form or as a spoken word impinging on my mind.

The information received in this manner, and also at a later date when engaged in chores requiring little concentration, always had a bearing on scientific, philosophic or religious material I had at some time read. These flashes of inspiration were always accompanied by a sensation of great exultation, which to me confirmed the truth of what I had received and tended to clarify the manner in which that particular piece of information fitted in with the whole.

Browsing through bookshops or libraries, my hand would sometimes automatically select a book, which by title, I would never consider reading. Flicking through the pages, my eye would glimpse maybe just a sentence which would be sufficient to bring enlightenment or confirmation of a certain line of thought. Through this gradual process I came to my own view of the manner in which science can produce the evidence relating man to his environment.

In various disciplines of science there exist the knowledge containing the evidence I present, but because of the nature of the conclusions which occur to any reasonably intelligent person of an open mind, science, due to a materialistic view of the universe, attempts to play down the work of those who are progressing towards the truth. The scientific data available today, if re-assessed in its proper context, could bring about a total re-appraisal of their view of the universe.

Several years after my mind commenced to expand under the influence of meditation, I read the various teachings of Silver Birch, the intelligence from the higher vibrations who communicated with this world through the mediumship of Maurice Barbanell. These teachings, I realised, confirmed in general terms the scientific understanding of the nature of the universe I had built up over a decade, revealing the fact that the universe and all within it are part of the One Supreme Intelligence which controls all forms and does not differentiate between race, colour or creed.

Having read my scientifically-based manuscript on the nature of the universe, Gordon Higginson, then President of the Spiritualists' National Union, suggested that it would be to some purpose to relate my view of the universe to the teachings of Silver Birch. This thesis is the result, and is offered with a view to stimulating discussion among those who pause and reflect on the manner in which the universe functions, the reason we are here and the future that lays before us. May the Great Spirit bless your deliberations.

Chapter one

Knowledge and faith

THE teachings of the various prophets which have given rise to the formation of religious denominations have always been biased to suit the interpretation placed upon those teachings by the instigators of each individual religion. These differences of opinions resulted in a continuing division of nations and the people within those nations.

The close alliance of State and Church brought about a situation whereby the teachings of the clergy of the religion to which one subscribed were utilised to suit the whims and aims of the State. Thus, what one would term "religion" tended to bring about a state of division among nations, their people and often families. All this because the simple teachings of the prophets were manipulated by man.

The improvement in the standard of education over the past century or so has lead to minds of a more enquiring nature to dispute much of the teachings of the various religious bodies. In some respects, this has not improved the standard of moral responsibility within our society, but one must place a large portion of the responsibility for this state of affairs fairly and squarely upon the shoulders of the clergy of those denominations who have for so long proclaimed teachings which were formulated many centuries ago and seldom questioned.

Thus, all teachings given to us for the purpose of developing our moral and spiritual welfare were delivered by those of a like nature to ourselves, good or bad, who professed a certain faith, and irrespective of whether they were right or wrong were prepared to expound on it. Fortunately, today we have made, in my estimation, sufficient progress of a scientific nature to enable us to realise the message of the prophets.

In conjunction with the progress of science, we have been fortunate in having, over recent years, a prophet — an inspired religious teacher or leader proclaiming God's will — who has brought us an updated version of the manner in which mankind can come to an understanding of the power we know as God.

These teachings have not come from our own level of consciousness, but been given to the world by a higher intelligence speaking through the entrancement of a developed human medium. The medium in question was Maurice Barbanell who, up to 1924, after studying many religions, declared himself an Atheist. However, in the course of investigating the phenomena of Spiritualism, he developed trance mediumship, which was the commencement of an association with an entity known as Silver Birch, who remained with him until the Barbanell's passing in July 1981.

This entity, with the blessing of Barbanell, took control of the physical body as and when required to do so, dispensed wisdom and knowledge, and presented an entirely different conception of the manner in which man relates to the universe, a feature of his teachings overlooked by even his closest friends.

His gentle approach to his task of appealing to the reason and judgement of mature, evolved, educated minds, in order to reveal the message of the Spirit in all its simplicity, was in stark contrast to the Evangelistic approach of the Orthodox church. He would say nothing that offended reason, would strive to manifest love, never reproach with anger and prove, by precept and example, that he was what he claimed to be, a messenger of what he would term "The Great Spirit."

Silver Birch imposed upon himself the burden of anonymity so it could not be said that he used title, rank or fame to enhance his teachings, but would be judged on what he said and what he did. Thus, because of this self-imposed condition, he was presented to our physical world as a representative of the North American Indian Race.

Never at any time did he claim authorship of the teachings he gave, but through transformation of vibrations (a subject I shall elucidate) acted merely as a messenger for those upon a higher level of consciousness. These teachings were kept simple, with continuous reference made to service to others and "the Law," which I would understand to be that of harmony, which, of course, incorporates love in its true context.

Because there is, as Silver Birch teaches, no limit to the knowledge available to mankind providing he has reached a stage of consciousness where he can attune his mind to receive advanced knowledge, through reasoning — a quality advocated in his teachings — surely a basis could be formed to establish a source of knowledge which could have an impact on society.

Like most of the religions, the Spiritualist movement has never been in a position to establish its claims on a scientific basis. However, I am confident that science has now reached the stage where it cannot deny any of the scientific background I provide for comprehending the teachings of Silver Birch. In the light of the research I have made into various aspects of many disciplines of scientific experiment, I have established to my own satisfaction the truth of the expression, "God is within everything," and the manner in which this applies.

To my mind, insufficient in-depth interest has been shown in his teachings with the consequence that much of what he taught has not been understood in its correct context. Therefore, through the inspiration I receive from time to time, I propose in as simple a manner as possible to provide substance to those teachings which in most cases have merely been glossed over through lack of knowledge.

All too often, the individual tends to read the teachings of Silver Birch as just another novel instead of realising that he is instructing them in the nature of the universe. Very few people have the interest to carry out research into this fascinating subject, but are content to read of the activities of others who are fortunate enough to possess gifts of a psychic nature. One cannot learn from the interests and the activities of others. One must take an active part in bringing one's own potential into play before one can derive any real satisfaction from one's interests.

Many will query why it is necessary to acquire knowledge when they possess faith. If one reflects on the following extract from Silver Birch's teachings you will note the warning contained therein: "Knowledge is always desirable. Knowledge should always be desirable. The one who stops and says 'I do not wish to know' is in effect demanding that he should become stultified, decayed and rusty. You cannot stand still. You must either advance or go back. You are travellers on an eternal march."

On the question of faith, Silver Birch speaks thus: "There are two important principles in life. One is knowledge, the other is faith. Faith without knowledge can be a very weak and even broken reed, but knowledge with faith is an admirable combination.

"You have knowledge which has brought comprehension of life and its meaning. You know it is only an infinitesimal part of knowledge that can be yours. Thus the element of faith must arise. But this is faith founded on knowledge. It is not the credulous faith, not the faith that insults the intelligence, but the faith founded on knowledge, that because of knowledge it is right to have faith."

Faith, therefore, must always precede knowledge for it is simply a question of the tangible physical world of which we are aware as related to the intangible nature of faith. Therefore, it is only by attuning our intangible minds to that of those functioning at a higher level of consciousness that we can obtain the knowledge that will bring about a greater understanding of the universe in which we live, and once acquired, bring about an upturn in the moral and spiritual nature of mankind. Silver Birch demonstrates this point in the following extract:

"I make bold to claim that almost every boon in your world, every invention and discovery, has its origin in the world of spirit. The minds of your world are but the receptacles of the greater minds who use them to confer new benefits to your world of matter."

Very gently, Silver Birch guides us through the path of knowledge that has always been available to us and reveals the responsibility that knowledge incurs:

"There is knowledge for all when you are ready to seek knowledge, but must journey on the great adventure. You must be prepared to start on a search where even the boundaries are not known. Sometimes be prepared for hazards and dangers; sometimes be prepared to walk in uncharted territory, yet always prepared to follow truth wherever she leads and reject all that is false, no matter how old it may be...

"There is no new truth. Truth is truth. There is knowledge which depends on the individual being ready to receive it. When you are children you are taught according to your capacity to assimilate. You begin with the letters of the alphabet and, as the mind grows, you are taught to make words and read.

"Gradually the knowledge contained in the printed word becomes accessible to you. As to the amount of knowledge you receive, that is dependent wholly and solely upon your capacity for appreciating it. There is an infinity of wisdom, range upon range upon range, but it can only become available to you as you are mentally and spiritually equipped to receive it.

"Once you display any initiative, and reveal by your actions and by your thoughts that you are ready and receptive, then you begin to harmonise and attune yourself with the processes which enable you to receive that knowledge and teaching for the stage you have reached. There are no final boundaries. There are no limits beyond which man cannot go for he is infinite, and knowledge is infinite, too.

"Before you learn, you must unlearn. You must discard all that which hinders your minds from thinking as they should. Thus your soul and spirit grow and you are ready for higher knowledge. You learn first of all to discard all that which is false, all that which makes your reason revolt, all that which is not in consonance with the love and the wisdom of the Great spirit.

"Learn to be free. Do not imprison yourself. Do not hedge yourself around and refuse to allow new inspiration to come to you. Truth is a constant search. Its boundaries are ever widening for as the soul evolves the mind responds.

"You become free when you realise there is no limitation

to knowledge, truth, wisdom, growth. You become free when you discard at once that which you know in your heart is false, that which reason rejects, because your intelligence cries out in revolt. You become free when you are not afraid to discard error in the face of new light.

"Personal guidance is a truth, but you have to be careful how you explain to the interested but yet uninitiated how it happens otherwise it would seem to them that you gain an unfair advantage in life merely because you have access to spiritual power.

"After all, the foundation of this truth is not that it enriches you materially but it enriches you spiritually, that it gives you a knowledge of laws and realities that provide a basis for a complete understanding of yourselves, the universe in which you dwell, and the Great Spirit, who is the divine architect.

"Your world needs this knowledge because it will illuminate the whole of life and make what was incomprehensible easy to understand. It will enable men to cease to be tortured by all the crudities and inadequacies of erroneous teachings that have for too long acted as a brake on progress.

"Some are not yet ready for this knowledge. Some think it unnecessary; others have to be treated like children, given toys with which to play until they can be led on to the paths where their minds will be instructed. I want you to get a comprehensive picture of the plan that lies behind all spirit teaching.

"It seeks to dissipate the darkness which has surrounded your world for so long, that has caused all the horrors with which you are becoming painfully familiar. At the root of all your evils is to be found this ignorance of spiritual law. Do you not realise that once the gospel of materialism and all the self-interest it teaches is exploded forever, you rid the world of its greatest curse?.

"You realise you are not creatures of chance, playthings of caprice, but part of the Infinite Spirit with an infinite power on which you can draw. Once this truth becomes universally accepted, once people fully realise that there is a world beyond the one of matter, that they are personally responsible for the lives they live, that there is an eternal law which operates with perfect justice, then you will have a new foundation for life.

"That is why we come back to your world...to ask you to give no obedience to any one man, to any one book, to any one church, to any being whether in the world of matter or in the world of spirit, but only to learn obedience to the laws of the Great Spirit, for they alone are infallible and unerringly right.

"That is why we emphasise the laws of the Great Spirit for the true understanding of these laws harmonises all knowledge. They cannot in any way cause the minds of scientists, philosophers, free-thinkers or anybody to revolt for they are founded upon eternal, unalterable, immutable operations of the Great Spirit.

"At any stage of evolution it is preferable that you should walk in the light rather than the darkness: it is better that you should be armed with knowledge rather than you should be swayed by ignorance. The pursuit of knowledge must always be one of the primary aims of all intelligent human beings otherwise superstition, prejudice, intolerance and bigotry would become rife were there not the demand for knowledge to counter them and to force them to retreat.

"At no time can you halt and say, 'Thus far will I go and no further.' There must always be the desire for education, for growth, for progress, for advancement, the attainment of the higher and the discarding of the lower.

"Knowledge brings responsibilities. It is part of the law of compensation. You have added to your mental stock something that you never before possessed, but, on the other side of the scale, there is the responsibility of what you do with that knowledge.

"You must not regard the power of the spirit as it was expressed in any period of man's history as being the final word in all divine revelation. Your world must realise that revelation is continuous and progressive, fitting itself to the stage of understanding of the people to whom it comes.

"It must only be so much in front that it is within their grasp. Always the power of the spirit is but one step ahead, and when man achieves that step, he is ready for the next in the infinite ladder of wisdom.

"Knowledge brings joy, happiness, serenity, but also brings responsibility as to what you do with that knowledge.

Knowledge will drive away many of the foolish fears that come with ignorance; knowledge will make you aware of yourself and what you should do now that you know, and you know that others are less fortunate. He who sins in ignorance pays the price, but he who sins with knowledge pays a greater price for his knowledge has increased his sin.

"What does happen is that sometimes there is a development of the brain, but not a development of the mind or the spirit, and then you have people who are intellectual, but it does not follow that because they are intellectual they are great souls or they have great minds.

"It is a progress that is limited strictly to the physical thing, the brain, and it is true that amongst those people there are those who reject anything but the complicated. But where there is true progress of the mind and the soul, then that progress brings a greater awareness of spiritual realities for it is a mental and spiritual development. In those cases you get a discarding of the former erroneous conceptions and a closer approximation to the truth.

"I want you to take from me the knowledge of what goes on behind physical life, all that vast power of the spirit which is surging around you, of the many influences for good which strive to use you.

"I want you to try to understand the potentialities of your own self so that you can have access to the vast armouries and riches of your own spiritual nature. I want you to realise that wisdom, divine wisdom, is inexhaustible, that the treasuries of the Great Spirit are infinite.

"I tell you with all the strength I can command that all of you who strive to serve have access to the greatest power in the universe, one that is life itself. It is a responsibility. Use it diligently, wisely.

"Help all who come within your orbit. If there are some with whom you cannot share this knowledge, let them go their way. Continue with the task as you see it according to your light and conscience. Motive determines all matters. If the motive is right, no matter what happens, you will emerge triumphant.

"Offer knowledge wherever you can. Sometimes it will be rejected and you will be met with scoffing, with ridicule, with mockery. That does not matter. It should not touch you. Those who are unready are perforce unreceptive, but you have done your task. But you will meet many to whom this will be precious drops of water when their souls are parched. Those are the ones that matter. If you help them, then at least you have justified your existence.

"Truth cannot enter closed minds. Truth can find a lodgement only when there is an ability to receive it. Truth, like the Great Spirit, is infinite. The amount you receive depends on your capacity. If you increase your capacity, you can receive more truth. You can never reach the stage where you know everything about the universe in which you dwell."

Within these extracts you have Silver Birch's teachings on the attainment of knowledge and the fact that if we are to progress we must assimilate knowledge available to us from a higher level of consciousness, free and *gratis*. It is merely a question of devoting time and patience in developing one's character and tuning in to the world of spirit.

The level at which one finds attunement with Spirit is dependent on the level of consciousness developed through the attitude of mind on a broad spectrum of subjects and interests which tend to form our character. Thus we find communication with spirit ranges from witch-doctors to those in receipt of higher teachings. I am unaware of the level at which my own nameless friends function, but it certainly is not of a nebulous nature.

In my estimation, the teachings of Silver Birch are on a level that the average human being can comprehend and provides the key that will give "you a knowledge of laws and realities that provide a basis for a complete understanding of yourself, the universe in which you dwell, and the Great Spirit, who is the divine architect." It will indeed "illuminate the whole of life and make what was incomprehensible easy to understand."

Silver Birch warns us, "Before you learn, you must unlearn." This applies in particular to the realms of science where "erroneous teachings have for too long acted as a brake on progress." Far too many of the teachings of Silver Birch were accepted purely from the point of view of turning the mind of mankind from the orthodox approach to the relationship of man to the universe towards an understanding of the natural laws predominating within our universe.

This knowledge of universal law has been available to us since the beginning of time. We must seriously consider whether we have been labouring under the burden of "erroneous teachings." Much work of a scientific nature is undertaken by those "of a development of the brain, but not a development of the mind or spirit. It does not follow because they are intellectual they are great souls or that they have great minds."

One of the problems in scientific research is the fact that there are many individual minds working within a single discipline in order to approach a common goal. Thus, there is seldom total agreement in any one particular field of research. Naturally, the majority line of thought prevails. Unfortunately, scientific research also tends to confine its interests within its own particular discipline. Those involved tend not to expand their minds in other directions.

Therefore, if we search through the work of those of a scientific bent who have been in a minority in their particular discipline, we are liable to locate the key to the universe which will make "that which was incomprehensible easy to understand."

It is only through science in conjunction with the inspiration from Spirit that can "give you knowledge of laws and realities that provides a basis for a complete understanding of yourselves, the universe in which you dwell, and the Great Spirit, who is the divine architect."

Science must rubber stamp any form of inspiration received from Spirit in order to substantiate any new laws arising, but once faith is established in the truth of that inspiration within the individual mind, that which has become truth to you becomes part of your eternal heritage.

The words of Silver Birch must be reiterated: "Truth cannot enter closed minds. Truth can only find lodgement when there is an ability to receive it. The amount you receive depends on your capacity. Truth is truth. There is knowledge which depends on the individual being ready to receive it."

In your search for truth, heed once more the words of Silver Birch: "You become free when you realise that there is no limitation to knowledge, truth, wisdom and growth. You become free when you discard at once that which you know in your heart is false, that which reason rejects, because your intelligence cries out in revolt. You become free when you are not afraid to discard error in the face of new light."

Therefore, in presenting my interpretation of the teachings of Silver Birch, I hope sincerely that you will meditate and reflect on my offering, for this is indeed the universe as I understand it, and coupled with the scientific research that has been placed in my hands by Spirit, represents to my satisfaction, true realty. The scientific data I present is in as simple terms as possible and fully supports, in my estimation, the teachings of Silver Birch.

Although but a small percentage of science as a whole would accept my prognosis, I place it before you to give you the opportunity of accepting or rejecting it, according to your level of consciousness.

The evidence is there, but due to the amount of research that has taken place over the last century or so, much of it has been forgotten in the constant search to satisfy the physical needs of mankind. The "spiritual" nature of the universe has been neglected, but perhaps I can provide more discerning readers with an answer that will provide them with the "knowledge of ourselves and the universe in which we live."

Through the acquisition of this knowledge, I find myself in a position where I must "Offer knowledge where you can. Sometimes it will be rejected and you will be met with scoffing, with ridicule and mockery." If I retain this knowledge for my own use, I can be accused of "not living in your lives the implications of the knowledge that has been vouchsafed to you."

The reason I must disseminate this knowledge is "to ensure that the children of the Great Spirit everywhere are enabled to build on true foundations that will endure amidst all the storms of life everywhere." This "knowledge brings joy, happiness, serenity, but also brings responsibility as to what you do with it. It is part of the law of compensation." At the same time, it will "drive away many of the foolish fears that come with ignorance."

My object in making this work as simple as possible,

without omitting the content, is to conform with Silver Birch's teaching that "It must not be so far ahead of them that they cannot understand it. It must only be so much in front that it is within their grasp. Each step forward means more understanding of life's purpose, its reality, the eternal principles on which it is founded, a greater perception of those eternal verities. With that comes closer attunement."

That we have progressed but little since Silver Birch enlightened us to the fact that "At the root of all your evils is to be found this ignorance of spiritual law" reflects little credit on the recipients of his teachings. This ignorance of spiritual law, which has always been within the grasp of mankind within the last half century or so, has resulted in a continuing moral decline of humanity.

Until we realise the implications attached to the knowledge of these laws, we shall never understand Silver Birch's communication, "That is why we emphasise the laws of the Great Spirit, for the true understanding of these laws harmonises all knowledge. They cannot in any way cause the minds of scientists, philosophers, free thinkers or anybody to revolt for they are founded upon eternal, unalterable, immutable operations of the Great Spirit." In the words of Silver Birch, "It is only by imbibing, by striving to get the complete picture, that life will be understood by you."

Apart from demonstrating the continuing existence of the spirit of man, little has been accomplished with regard to research into the facets of knowledge sprinkled throughout the teachings of Silver Birch. These should have acted as an impetus to raise us to the next level of "understanding of yourselves, the universe in which you dwell and the Great Spirit, who is the divine architect."

The teachings of Silver Birch are orientated towards taking the whole of mankind that one step further on the path to the realisation of our relationship to the universe. It is not a teaching that takes us into the realms of fantasy, to which many are addicted.

If we do not now have an understanding of the true nature of the universe, how can one, within the bounds of reason, comprehend the loosely termed "higher teachings" which are abroad today? Let us imbibe further teachings when we reach our next level of consciousness.

Aided by the teachings of Silver Birch, philosophers, scientific research and the relationship between these knowledgeable sources obtained during meditative periods of time, I will endeavour to present a view of the universe which appeals to my reason and understanding.

Following in the footsteps of Silver Birch, I align myself with his words, "People like myself have been entrusted with trying to tell the truth about the spiritual life, not in any mystical sense as the phrase so often conveys, but what it is in reality."

May I commend to you the words of Silver Birch: "You are all eternal pilgrims on an eternal march. Your equipment you must select with reason, common sense and intelligence to guide you. You will find part of your equipment in books and in many lives.

"Therefore, you should select that which appeals to you, not because somebody else said it is good, or wise, or sacred, or should be reverenced, but only because it is helpful to you on your journey."

Chapter two

Spirit — the architect of matter

HOW many individuals have, in the course of reading the teachings of Silver Birch, paused to consider the following extracts and realised the implications attached to them?

"Matter itself has no existence. Matter exists because it is activated by the spirit."

"Spirit is superior to matter. Spirit is king and matter the servant. Spirit reigns supreme. It is the essence out of which all life is made for spirit is life and life is spirit."

"Primarily man is a spirit with a body, not a body with a spirit. The body is subservient to the spirit."

"Matter only exists because of spirit. Spirit is the eternal reality. Spirit is indestructible, imperishable, immortal, infinite."

"Nowhere in the world of matter do you have the hallmark of reality because matter depends on spirit for its existence. Matter is but one manifestation in one form of vibration of spiritual reality. You are spiritual beings with material bodies. The eternal reality is the spirit, not the physical body."

"The troubles of your world are largely due to the fact that materialism dominates the actions and thoughts of millions of people. Greed and avarice are the malignant cancers that infect your plane. These have to be driven out by knowledge, by understanding, by the fundamental truth that all life is founded on spirit and not matter."

"By ordering your lives in harmony with this knowledge,

you automatically have at your disposal everything that is essential for your well-being, spiritually, mentally and physically. It is the thought that is wrong in allowing physical things to predominate too much."

The substance of these extracts are to the effect that the fundamental truth is that matter and life itself are dependant upon spirit. This means that the whole structure of the universe, from the smallest particle of matter to the masses which constitute the universe, are a product of spirit.

To the materialistic scientists — and indeed the majority of the population of this world — the idea that our material world is subservient to a form of energy beyond our five senses is an absolute nonsense. However, there are within the ranks of the scientists small groups and individuals who are pushing back the self-imposed barriers of prejudice. Although they are unaware of the fact, they are in the process of proving the truth that, as Silver Birch teaches, "matter is a product of spirit."

This teaching is the key to "illuminate the whole of life and make what was incomprehensible easy to understand." Once we accept this teaching, we have access to further research into the nature of the universe. The immediate benefits will be a more informed view of the nature of mankind, the manner in which the universe functions and new methods of medical treatment through the spirit rather than the physical body.

A thorough scientific investigation into the nature of Silver Birch's spirit will promote a fresh attitude of mind within the whole of humanity. The realisation that we all stem from the same source to which we return, that the whole of the universe is subject to natural law, and the "supernatural" is no more, will bring about the understanding that we are all "part of the whole," irrespective of race, colour or creed, and should therefore move forward together in complete harmony.

Once we fully comprehend the true nature of birth and death in terms of scientific research perhaps we shall, between those periods of time, come to understand our personal commitment to humanity and the universe at large. Confirmation of the eternal nature of the spirit of mankind should act as a spur to a more harmonious existence between man, nations and the environment.

Placed on a firm scientific basis, this natural law "cannot cause the minds of scientists, philosophers, free-thinkers or anybody to revolt." The pieces are all in place: it is up to the world of science to complete the jigsaw in order that the knowledge may be assimilated by those mentally less equipped. Unfortunately, although truth is placed before the eyes of these men of science, their materialistic instincts will not allow them to accept anything of an intangible nature when the choice is between that and the physical structure of matter.

Such is the choice facing those who conduct experiments within the auric field of we humans. How can these experimenters specifically state that the physical body is responsible for reactions noted within the field of the aura?. It is just as valid to state that the auric field produces reaction in the physical body. This is the area where a link has been established between the physical body of matter and the energy field surrounding it.

The description of spirit given by Silver Birch relates to the energy fields surrounding matter in the following manner: "The power of the spirit is invisible. It does not conform to any of the recognised standards of man. It has no length, it has no breadth, it has no colour, it has no size, it has no taste, it has no smell."

However, it does conform to one recognised standard of man in that it can, today, be investigated in terms of electrical measurements. Dr E.K Muller in researching the nature of the auric field concluded that:

1. The field is not electrical in nature as we understand the term, but can be measured in terms of electromagnetic dynamics.

2. The field can change non-conductors to conductors.

3. The field can pass through glass, mica, copper and tinfoil.

4. The field can be varied in strength by the rate and quality of the blood circulating around the physical body. Quality depends on food, drink or physical exercise. Willpower also influences strength of field

This data has only been included for the benefit of the

initiated and can be ignored by the majority of readers. It simply means that we do have the equipment today to investigate the phenomena of the auric field.

Silver Birch rather confuses the issue in his interpretation of the auric field in which he states, "The aura consists of the vibrations set up by the body." This contradicts his previous statements that the spirit is responsible for producing matter. One can state with confidence that it is only within the auric field that any form of spirit can be identified which would be capable of influencing the production of matter.

However, I do agree that "There are many auras, but the ones that are known to your world are the auras that surround the physical body and the spiritual body. All things have auras, even things which do not have consciousness within them."

The description of the auric field provided by White Eagle is given in a more detailed manner, and with the application of a little elementary science appeals to reason. White Eagle speaks of five separate bodies being present in the human aura, which to some degree concurs with Silver Birch's remarks regarding "the auras that surround the physical body and the spiritual body."

The manner in which these "bodies" can be identified as separate units existing within close proximity is by each "body" functioning on different frequencies, vibrations or wavelengths. Thus, we have within the aura an energy field identified by science as being electromagnetic in nature, and "functioning in the ultra-violet, visible and infrared ranges." It can therefore be reasonably assumed that multiple "bodies" at varying electromagnetic ranges exist within the auric field, which confirms the teachings received.

By the very nature of the auric field, "one field cannot exist within another field without interaction taking place and producing results of great significance." Applied to the field of the aura, this simply means that any change of frequency, vibration or wavelength within one "body" is reflected in similar terms in the related "bodies" or fields.

Silver Birch describes the Great Spirit as "the natural law of the universe. The Great Spirit is the creative force behind all life, whether registered in the plane of matter or the plane of spirit. The Great Spirit's infinite intelligence planned the whole of the universe and devised immutable laws for its governance." I would submit that this description of the Great Spirit cannot in any way offend the conception of the God of the Orthodox religions of the world.

Professor Albert Einstein expresses the attitude of the scientist to religion in the following terms: "His religious feeling takes the form of a rapturous amazement at the harmony of natural law, which reveals an intelligence of such superiority that, compared with it, all the systematic thinking and acting of human beings is an utterly insignificant reflection."

Therefore, all matter must be directed by intelligence in whatever form it may take. Through the research carried out by various scientists, and recorded by Dr Helmut Breithaupt, a process known as holography could be the means whereby "the entire spatial information of an object (matter) can be stored and then reconstructed again" within the field of the aura.

A further feature of the holographic nature of the auric field is that every fragment of the individual auric field possesses the essential characteristics of the complete field. This is the principle behind our present-day forensic testing of blood and semen. The most minute spot of fluid, or indeed portion of an individual body, carries with it a complete pattern of the auric field which controls the DNA of that individual body.

Research by scientists such as Professor H.R. Burr and Dr Inyushin designate the auric field as the matrix or mould of the physical body of matter.

Further to this, Professor Burr informs us that these fields are "responsible for the maintenance of the human body by controlling the rebuilding and replacement of molecules and cells in the precise pattern of the original." We can therefore accept that they are stating that the DNA control of the physical form of a body stems from the electromagnetic nature of the auric field surrounding it.

Summing up the nature of the auric field, as discussed, we field the following:

1. The auric field is the product of multiple individual

fields functioning at various ranges of electromagnetic energy.

2. The auric field is holographic in nature, providing the means of storing and retrieving information and providing identification by division.

3. Change of the electromagnetic range of an individual field, interacting with other fields of a similar nature, can produce reaction within those fields.

One may therefore conclude that the spirit of Silver Birch is an intelligence working through electromagnetic fields.

Chapter three

Spirit within the aura

OUR perception of the auric field at the present time has been limited to the extent that it can be observed by a suitably endowed clairvoyant as a radiation, ranging in colour from dirty red to purple, egg-shaped in form, surrounding the physical body. The inner radiations of colour appear to be pretty stable while the outer ones of a more nebulous nature reflect emotional states.

From observation of the aura, one can draw inferences as to the emotional state or character of the individual by means of the colours generated within its field. The colours within the aura are interpreted as follows:

Brilliant red, anger and force; dirty red, passion and sensuality; brown, avarice; rose, affection; yellow, high-type intellectual activity; purple, spirituality; blue, religious devotion; green, deceit and jealousy, and, in a deeper shade, sympathy. Further to this, the clairvoyant who reads the aura can perceive signs within the field of adverse health conditions.

Semyon Kirlian in his experiments with his high voltage/ frequency photography confirmed the interpretation of the colours prevailing within the aura and also the value of studying the field for medical diagnosis.

Medical research programmes were initiated spanning the lifetime of a group of people, and much research carried out in the field of agriculture.

We have previously referred to each of the several individual electromagnetic fields within the aura functioning at various frequencies, vibrations or wavelengths. If we relate frequency/vibration to wavelength in the colour spectrum, one can comprehend that the colours present in the auric field are entirely due to the frequency/vibrations present within the field of the aura.

The influence of change of frequency/vibration in one of the fields, being of an electromagnetic nature, would, through interaction with fields of a similar nature, produce a change of colour within the auric field. Taking as an example the changing thoughts passing through one's mind, one can readily imagine the fluctuating colours present within the field. The more deep-seated thoughts which gives an individual his character are registered in the more stable area of the aura.

Silver Birch provides us with a little more information on the nature of the universe, which of course, includes the physical body. He stated: "We speak of vibration in terms of energy...Everything that exists vibrates, radiates and is active." Bearing this statement in mind, much of our research into the aura will be on these lines.

Let us now go a little further along the path and explore the description of the aura provided by White Eagle, and the manner in which it functions.

The field first mentioned by White Eagle is the vital body. He refers to this as "an aura of a few inches, and of a bluish colour, emanating from the physical body." What he sees (the clairvoyant) is the vital life-force (spirit) interpenetrating the physical body, which is used as a medium between the spiritual and the earth life (matter). This illustrates the relationship existing between spirit (intelligence functioning through electromagnetic energy) and matter. Once again, White Eagle makes the same error as Silver Birch in speaking of "emanations from the physical body" for this contradicts their teachings. However, the relationship between spirit and matter is so close that it is excusable error, as I will explain in later passages.

First we must recap on the nature of the fields of the aura, namely that its "holographic properties provide the means of storing and retrieving information." One can therefore assume that in all respects the fields can be equated to a computer, which as Burr and Inyushin suggest, acts as the matrix or mould of the physical body.

The next stage is to establish the method by which this information is exchanged between the field (spirit) and the physical body, which obviously takes us back to the world of science. Professor Herbert König and Dr Walter Kroy are in complete agreement with the following approach to the relationship between the fields and matter:

"These fields provide electromagnetic signals which are short enough to penetrate the skin structure with moderate absorption in selected areas of the body surface. These signals appear to be responsible for fundamental regulatory functions by passing information through the contact regions to the organ cells via the connecting tissue, and the organs in turn, using a similar system, communicate internally."

From the perception of Vera Stanley Alder in "The Initiation of The World," this function is described in the following terms: "Where great activity and condensed structures in the etheric body (auric field) is located we get a plexus — a close lattice work of nerves forming a nucleus — and at the heart of the nucleus we find in the etheric body a vital vortex, or 'centre,' which is expressed in the flesh as an endocrine gland.

"When seen with the etheric sight, the etheric body looks like a phosphorescent cobweb sewn with stars — the centres. When seen with the astral sight an entirely different appearance comes in to view.

"The atoms of the astral body are minute, crystal-shaped, scintillating and coloured, and usually, in constant swirling movement. They pass outwards from the centre of the body to the periphery of the astral body, flow around it and converge inwards again — a constant rotary movement. The commencement of this rotary movement is around the centres, which appear as little revolving vortices."

Through clairvoyant vision we thus establish the fact that the energy centres of the aura are concentrated in the area of the pineal, pituitary, thyroid, thymus, pancreas, adrenal and gonad glands which constitute the endocrine system and are responsible for the balanced maintenance of the physical body. Esoteric teachings refer to these areas as the "chakras." I would imagine the closing of these vital areas would cause more than a few problems for the uninitiated.

In his experiments with leaves from trees and bushes, Kirlian found that healthy leaves, when photographed, revealed a "brilliant array of twinkling lights" surrounding them, and forming the aura. On removing a section of leaf by cutting, it was found that the original complete field of the aura persisted.

One must therefore agree that this rather simple experiment demonstrates that the mould or matrix (spirit) remains intact at all times until physical death. This condition was witnessed by Kirlian as he "observed the final flicker of flame as the aura departed from a dying leaf."

This phenomenon is substantiated by Dr Bernhard Ruth, who states that "the death of grain seedlings is indicated by a sudden rise in photon emission. The question therefore arises of whether an increased emission of photons always accompanies the death of living beings."

The term "photon emission" reveals the fact that science regards matter as the only source of phenomena associated with it, and all research is confined to that area. Common sense would in that case dictate that the level of photon emission would decrease rather than increase on the death of living matter.

Ruth then continues his discourse in the following terms, "The processes controlling photon emission are responsible for the reaction rate in the interior of cells."

Dr Helmut A Fischer adds his comments to this statement, "It is possible and thinkable, however, that photons, i.e. physically related quanta, act as regulators of cytobiological processes e.g. by influencing the operator molecules from which we know from genetics."

Professor Popp introduces fresh terminology relating to the same process, "Thus, there is solid evidence that DNA works really as a photon store," which is substantiated by Z. Zhen and X. Shan from the Chinese Academy of Sciences, Beijing.

Professor Popp continues his discourse: "DNA — sequence — specific biophoton transfer appears as likely. It could well provide the molecular basis of immunological activity, repair functions and genetic control like transcriptions and replication of DNA."

Once again scientists have reversed the process of operation due to their absorbing interest in matter. They have reached the right conclusion with regard to the relationship between the photon and the physical body, but as yet have not accepted that the photon is the storage and delivery system which controls the DNA of animate and inanimate matter, not *vice versa.*

In reply to material I forwarded to Professor Popp on this aspect of the auric field he commented:

"Thank you for your pages on the light patterns of the human body. Possibly you are right with your ideas about it. It is very interesting to see again the connection between research results and the ancient traditional medicine." I think something must have got lost in the translation, for the research results were related to White Eagle's interpretation of the auric field.

When one observes the amount of theoretical mathematical calculations that have been postulated in approaching this stage of scientific research into the phenomena of the aura, one can appreciate Silver Birch's comment that "The issues are always so simple, but the people of your world do not like simplicity. They like form and convention; they like to copy and imitate."

Science must go through its ritual of the time honoured process of expending mental energy on mathematical calculation instead of accepting the teaching of Silver Birch that "You strive through aspiration and attunement to establish unity with that power. Your prayer should always be a desire for more illumination, knowledge, wisdom and understanding."

By combining the intellect of the scientist with an appropriate approach to spirit, maybe life upon earth could be revitalised. The philosophers of old, without all the modern aids available to science today, were far more aware of the true nature of the universe than the average scientist is today.

Returning to the subject of the vital field of the aura, I do not consider we have much difficulty in accepting that the "phosphorescent cobweb sewn with stars," "the brilliant array of twinkling lights" and "photons" are one and the same thing, the source providing the information necessary for the DNA to control the form and maintenance of a specific physical body.

The manner in which Silver Birch and White Eagle assume that the field of the aura is an emanation of the physical body is best explained by the process of procreation of all life, and in particular, the human being.

As mentioned previously, the male sperm, in a fluid state, is — because of the holographic nature of the auric fields of the male — surrounded by a complete replica of the vital field pattern of the male aura. In exactly the same manner, the egg of the female carries a replica of the vital field pattern of the aura of the female. When the head of the sperm penetrates egg membrane, the nucleus of egg and sperm fuse, providing the chromosomes and genes the carry for mitotic cell division.

At the instant of the fusing of egg nucleus and sperm, the vital field patterns of male and female fuse. The resulting vital field pattern takes control of the newly-formed embryo producing, in time, a child that in general has the physical attributes, or otherwise, of both parents.

Thus, because the fusing of physical matter and spirit (intelligence functioning through electromagnetic energy) is simultaneous, one can easily be deceived.

However, if one bears in mind Silver Birch's words that "matter only exists because of spirit," then one can only conclude that the newly-formed Vital field pattern, equipped with its multitudinous array of star-like photons, provides information for the control of the chromosomes and genes of the embryo.

Silver Birch speaks of the relationship between matter and spirit in the following terms: "Do not divide the life of matter from that of spirit...The body of matter is dependent on the body of spirit for its existence, but the body of spirit is dependent on that of matter for presentation." One may also add a further comment of Silver Birch, "The power of the spirit is the garment of the soul."

At the time of conception — and prior to the actual birth of the child — only two of the five fields of which White Eagle speaks are utilised as it is only a question of producing matter over a period of time, and does not require the presence of the incarnating entity. The physical structure of the embryo is entirely undertaken by the computer-like vital field.

Silver Birch refers to the initiation of spirit into the physical world of matter in the following terms: "As spirit you have always existed, because spirit is part of life and life is part of spirit. You have always existed. Because you are part of the Great Spirit, which is the life force, you have never had a beginning, but you as an individual, as a separate, conscious individuality, must begin somewhere, even in the stream of life.

"When conception takes place, the cells of the male and female meet and provide a vehicle for a particle of the life force to begin to express itself through a physical body. The life force is unexpressed until there is a vehicle through which it can manifest.

"That is what the earth parents provide. From the time the cells have coalesced and form their union, the tiny particle of spirit has naturally attached itself and begins its expression in your world of matter...

"What you call conception means that there is life. If there is no conception, there is no life. Therefore, spirit incarnates into matter at the moment of conception. As to the question of its development, this is more difficult because it depends on a variety of circumstances. The spirit that incarnates at the moment of birth has always existed as spirit...

"From the moment of conception there is life and there is spirit. If there is what you call in your world a miscarriage or an abortion, you have not destroyed the life force. You have merely removed its expression from your world to ours."

The terminology is rather confusing, but in essence Silver Birch is confirming my own description of the process of birth. If we take the sentence, "From the time the cells coalesced and formed their union, the tiny particle of spirit has naturally attached itself and begins its expression in your world of matter," one can perceive that it is a description of the one process.

Here we have the coalescing of the cells which provide the genes and chromosomes and "the tiny particle of spirit" — the immutable, intelligent force which constitutes the natural law of the universe, which shapes and maintains all matter in its various forms — "which naturally attaches itself and begins its expression in your world." At this stage we have a physical embryo which is on a par with the animal species and obviously a living creature.

It is not until "The spirit that incarnates at the moment of birth" enters the auric field that the embryo becomes a human being. As this particular spirit "has always existed," it is obviously the incarnating entity.

Thus, in the event of a miscarriage or abortion, the "tiny particles of spirit" can no longer function and depart. "The spirit that incarnates at the moment of birth" appears at delivery, and upon finding unfavourable conditions, returns to the world of spirit.

Once that spiritual link has been established between the field energies of the mother and the intending incarnate entity, I feel that it is never broken. If an opportunity arises at a later date, that same entity will take advantage of it. If not, and the spiritual tie remains strong, that same entity will be there to greet the parents on transition.

Chapter four

The fields of character

"ALL life is one life, but it has many graduations Man is more than matter. Man is mind and spirit, and there are vibrations that belong to the mental and spiritual life. In addition, there are vibrations which belong to the super-physical life, the life that is beyond the earthly world.

"Man can register the vibrations of this life in which he lives, and the vibrations of that larger life which one day will be his eternal habitat...There is the body of matter, the body of spirit and the vital cord or lifeline between."

These passages are from the teachings of Silver Birch. If one accepts that spirit is intelligence functioning through electromagnetic energy — and that vibrations (fields) within the aura are capable of storing and retrieving information as required — we have been presented with a pretty comprehensive picture of the content of the life-giving power which surrounds and sustains us.

Your character — soul — depends on the level of vibration at which the various fields of the aura function. Levels of vibration are largely controlled by the thoughts generated within the mind of the individual, through the five senses of the physical body.

One must bear in mind that by their very nature, these fields exist in a similar manner to radio signals which work on differing frequencies/vibrations. As you will probably have observed when listening on a certain wavelength, one occasionally gets interference from a source functioning on a rather different frequency/vibration. This is what one would term interaction between differing levels of frequency/vibration. It depends on the strength of the signal generated within the respective fields as to which prevails in establishing changes in frequency/vibration within either or any adjacent fields.

You will realise as we study the aura further the manner in which frequencies/vibrations within the energy fields affect us both physically and mentally in interacting with each other. White Eagle gives us an example of interaction when he speaks of qualities of the vital field:

"This particular aura, the etheric or vital body, is closely connected with the nervous system, and collects most of what later manifests as ill-health of the physical body, holding fast to poisons put forth by the lower mind of man by wrong thinking, wrong eating, and wrong living." Once we comprehend the fact that energy fields within the aura continually react to each other, we can then perceive the manner in which our character (soul) is developed.

Continuing our examination of the human aura, as described by White Eagle, we are introduced to the field in close proximity to the physical body, which is described in the following manner:

"Attached to the physical body is a certain form recognisable as the body elemental. This is not an evil thing; it has its place in the evolution not only of man, but also of the lower forms of life. We have been asked how it is that when man is in a physical body the pull of evil seems so much stronger than the attraction, the aspiration to good. You will find the answer in this body, or desire elemental, which is very strong in most men.

"Man has to learn in the course of his evolution that the higher self (which is only partially in evidence in most of us) must gain complete domination over the body elemental...But the body elemental is also assisting man in his evolution, as a kind of ballast which keeps him tied to earth.

"You all feel this pull, but it is not to be regarded as evil for it forces growth of the spiritual or God-consciousness which we all come back on earth to unfold."

This field is obviously of a more negative nature which attracts the mind — through interaction — towards the lower ranges of frequency/vibration which would relate to the dirty red area of the aura observed by a suitably developed medium.

This, then, is the source of the lower animal, like desires and sexual drive, present within the mind of mankind, which we are exhorted to overcome during our sojourn upon the earth plane. It is not evil in the sense that it is required for procreation in order that others from spirit may reincarnate to fulfil their destinies.

We all possess free will. It is a question of whether we allow the negative field of the body elemental to dominate the energy field of the mind — or *vice versa* — which is our own free choice. The path of spiritual progress lies in raising the vibrations of the mind; the influx of the lower vibrations of the body elemental should be resisted.

The vital body and the body elemental form the auric field of the pre-natal embryo, and via the vital cord, which possesses the same attributes as the respective fields, provides, by photon control, signals to the respective areas of the brain, where the vital cord terminates. The particular areas of the brain which complement the properties of these particular energy fields are, according to Stuart Sutherland on his research into the function of the brain, as follows.

The hind-brain and cerebellum, "which is responsible for the basic reflexes and is similar to the brain of a reptile," relates to the vital field of the aura. The hypothalamus, like that of the brain of lower mammals, controls the sex drive and emotions, equating to the body elemental.

White Eagle next describes the astral body as follows: "The astral body is that usually seen by clairvoyants, who will describe the aura and say it has certain colours...If the body elemental is very strong, holding great power, the astral aura will be coarse. Consequently, the colours will be coarse rather than beautiful.

"When the soul can recognise the reality of the spirit life and the purpose of its incarnation, then this astral body will grow finer and the colours more beautiful...The astral body of the ordinary person, as we have said, can range from dull, murky colours, misty and indefinite, to a very beautiful, well formed aura, egg-like in shape, composed of definite and harmonious colours."

Apart from the changing colours and the quality and brilliance of the astral field, there is little information provided by White Eagle on the function of this particular field.

However, if we consider the experiences of Sylvan Muldoon, a projector of the astral body with whom Hereward Carrington co-operated in revealing the vital part it plays in our present incarnation, we shall have a much better idea of the manner in which we relate to the universe. Muldoon concentrates in particular on the vital cord during astral projection in the following extracts:

"The cord centres at a given plexus...The ideal spot is the medulla oblongata, which has direct control over the organs of respiration in the oblivious physical body...This vital structure is composed, so far as I am able to see, of the same material, or essence, as the astral body itself.

"When slightly out of coincidence (moving away from its normal situation about the body) the cord is the diameter of a silver dollar. This is the maximum calibre of the cord itself yet the aura surrounding it gives the impression to the eye that it is about six inches in thickness at this point. It is in appearance of a whitish grey colour, and when greatly extended, is not unlike a long single strand of cobweb.

"From coincidence to the end of cord activity range there is always a double action taking place in the cord, that is, as far as one's eyes can determine...

"One is a regular pulsating action. The other appears to be a slight expansion and contraction of the outstretched organ...Each throb of the heart can be felt in the astral; each throb is expressed throughout the cable; each throb produces a beat in the physical heart. All three are simultaneous.

"One cannot only feel the heart's pulsations in his astral head, but he can feel them by touching the cable with his astral hand, just as you feel your physical pulse with your physical hand.

"Each breath taken in the astral can be seen pulsing over the astral cord and causing a duplicate breath to be taken in the insensible body. When consciously projected, one can suspend his breath at will, just as he can when in coincidence...The instant it is suspended, the before mentioned action of slight expansion and contraction ceases, in the psychic cable, as it likewise does in the physical body; but while the respiration ceases, the regular pulsating action continues.

"A deep breath in the astral will produce an identical breath in the physical body; a short one will produce a short one; a quick one will produce a quick one, etc. You breath in the astral and your heart beats in the astral just as it does when you are in coincidence. Your physical heart beats because within it the astral heart beats....

"That is the purpose of the astral 'Line of force,' to deliver the 'Breath of life' to the physical body...It is the astral entity which is the real 'You.' It is the universal energy that is the breath of life."

Obviously, as these observations were made while the operator was consciously projected in the astral body, contact between all other faculties of the physical body were maintained, even if not visible, to the operator's astral eye. Therefore, one can accept that the field of the astral body is the real "You," and that the physical body responds to its promptings.

We can now more fully comprehend the further passage of White Eagle on the astral body: "While on earth you are building your auras, contributing through your desires to the astral body, and through the astral to the mental and celestial bodies. You are building that celestial body by your actions and reactions, your thoughts and desires."

This seems logical if we are aware that as we progress spiritually through the influence of the five senses of our physical body functioning in an environment of matter, our way of thinking changes.

Thus, as "like attracts like," the higher we raise our own consciousness, the higher level of consciousness we attract to our celestial body. A medium would probably describe this situation as "a change of guides."

Silver Birch seeks to explain the phenomenon where the body we perceive at any stage of spiritual development is subject to a similar body functioning at a higher frequency/vibration, as follows:

"You live and move and breathe, you think and reflect,

you decide and judge, you ponder and consider, because of the power of the spirit. You see and hear, you move and walk, you think and talk, because of the power of the spirit. All that you do, all that you are, is due to the power of the spirit for your whole world of matter, and your body of matter, is dependent upon that vital, energising influx of spirit which gives it being, purpose, direction and life.

"You have an etheric body which reproduces its physical counterpart, but this does not contain muscles, gastric juices or an auditory system. The etheric counterpart is the intervening envelope for the spirit to manifest and function efficiently through the physical body. When death comes, the etheric has served its primary purpose as the vehicle for the soul to continue its next phase.

"The etheric is sloughed off and another body replaces it. The process of refinement requires more spiritual vehicles for expression. You can have many bodies...

"The whole purpose of life is evolution, growth, attainment. As you evolve, so automatically you discard the body which has served its purpose and assume the one that is fitted for your stage of evolution.

"You have many bodies manifesting at varying rates. When you slough off the physical body you take on the etheric counterpart, which you have always had, and express yourself through it because that has the proper rate of vibration to enable you to function. That is all as real to the etheric as to your physical body is to you while you are on earth.

"You have many bodies; you can call them astral, etheric and spirit. You manifest in the body which is capable of expressing the state you have reached. When you evolve to another stage, you shed that body like the caterpillar does. You express yourself in the form suitable for your latest development. This is how it works. It is infinite progression.

"The world is part of the astral world because all worlds are interpenetrating. All stages of life throughout the whole of the universe mingle and merge into one another and spiritual, astral, physical are varying aspects of one universal life. At this very moment you are registering in the physical world and in the spiritual world all at the same time.

"All life is one life with infinite gradations. You are as

much in the next world as ever you will be. It is only a question of the rate of your vibration. You are as much a spiritual being now as ever you will be...Death will not transform you into a spiritual being; death will not enhance your spiritual stature by one iota.

"You are spirit; you always were spirit; you always will be spirit. At present you are aware of that portion of spirit which is manifested in a physical body. As you evolve after what is called death, more and more of the unexpressed spirit will be able to display itself, but the spirit has never gone anywhere, it has never come from anywhere. It always was, it always is, it always will be.

"If you are aware that you are a spiritual being with a body, that your world is not your permanent abode, that everything physical is ephemeral...If you are aware that you, the indestructible you, the you that is divine, will emerge after death to continue the life of infinite progress...

"Then if you are wise, you will behave in such a fashion that automatically you prepare for what is your future existence beyond death. Your actions will be governed by the stage of spiritual awareness you have reached."

Summing up the nature of the astral body, we can express it in terms of the controlling spiritual counterpart of the physical body, functioning on a frequency/vibration appropriate to the level of consciousness attained in the course of actions and reactions to environmental conditions and experiences within the frequency/vibration of our world of matter.

Speaking on the subject of the aura, of which the astral field predominates — due to the fact that it is the product of the influence generated in the associated fields — Silver Birch reminds us that all knowledge assimilated through the five senses is stored and retrieved as necessary within the aura. He stated:

"Those who can see the aura and interpret them know all the secrets of the individual...They know the state of his soul and his mind's unfoldment. They can tell the evolution of that soul for it is the aura that enables you to be read like an open book.

"Your aura registers all that you have said, all that you

have thought and all that you have done. Your aura is your eternal judgement for there you are showing to those who can see exactly what you are within and not as you show yourself without."

Therefore, as Silver Birch reminds us, "There is not a man seated on a great white throne" to pass judgement upon us. We, during the course of our sojourn upon the earth plane, through our experiences of life, registered within our personal auric field, become our own judge and jury. The next stage of evolution of the spirit is determined by the level of spiritual awareness in terms of frequency/vibrations ("rate of your vibration").

Thus, those that have acquired an aura within the range of black, dirty red, grey or brown will find their future plane of existence, or "mansion," within that particular range of frequency/vibrations.

Likewise, individuals with auras in the frequency/vibration range of the blues and purples will also find their future existence in planes of a similar frequency/vibration. "Like attracts like." Therefore, irrespective of the frequency/vibration our astral body attains during its sojourn upon the earth plane, that is the plane of existence one is automatically attracted to on transition.

The field or body, which establishes the overall frequency/vibration of the astral body, is that which White Eagle refers to as follows.

"Extending again beyond the astral aura can be seen a similar egg-shaped form, but of finer, more ethereal matter. This is the aura of the mental body. It also can change rapidly with changing thoughts. Beyond and interpenetrating this to a fine degree is the aura of the celestial or heavenly body, of beautiful form, and colours almost impossible to describe, because their earth equivalent is hardly known.

"To this celestial body or aura, the ego of man finally withdraws after he has passed through the experiences of earth, of the astral body, including the Summerland, and of the mental life. All these conditions of life can only be contacted through your corresponding auras."

This field, aura or body of the mind must be that of the incarnating entity for it is only through the thoughts generated within the mind of the individual which can raise or lower the frequency/vibration, by interaction of the remaining fields of the aura. The "life forces" within the fields of the vital and body elemental are limited in the levels at which they function, but the field of the mind, because it possesses free will, can fluctuate from the higher range of frequency/ vibrations, where it is in closer association with the celestial field, down to the level of the body elemental, which sustains the lower nature of man.

One can therefore realise that until one possesses a settled, positive mind, the astral field is at the mercy of every little whim of the mental field.

Discarnate entities, communicating all their intimate little details from their differing planes of existence through mediumship, leave no doubt that these entities still retain the field of the mind intact. It is, therefore, not too difficult to accept that this field of the mind is the evolving, eternal spirit, which, if orientated in a positive manner through harmony and service to others, can draw ever closer to the Universal Architect.

The fields of the vital, body elemental and celestial bodies, combined with the free will incorporated in the field of the mind, develop the character of that particular spirit. Very much like a robot, the brain is merely the transmitter/receiver of the physical body.

The mind is the operator. Signals of a photon nature are received from the brain in response to reactions of the five senses, and signals are dispatched to the brain to instruct the same five senses to carry out the bidding of the mind.

The astral cord provides the means of conveying this constant flow of information along with similar signals from the vital and body elemental fields, providing the brain with the necessary data for the automatic functions of the body. One can therefore fully understand Silver Birch's comment that "Once the silver cord is severed and the connection between the physical and spirit has gone, there is no more animation" of the physical body.

As I previously suggested, the knowledge of the universe possessed by ancient philosophers was far in advance of that generally accepted today.

In Ecclesiastes 12, 6-7, this question of the parting of the physical and spirit is spoken of in the following terms: "Or ever the Silver cord be loosed, or the Golden bowl be broken, or the pitcher be broken at the fountain, or the Wheel be broken at the cistern. Then shall the dust return to the earth as it was and the Spirit return to God who gave it."

Professor H.S Burr, in his research into "life fields," approached the subject of the mind in the following manner: "In the meantime, we should remember the fact — pointed out by Sir Charles Sherrington several decades ago — that the mind of man does not exist in time, does not occupy space, and involves, so far as anyone knows, no energy transformations. But the nervous system, through which the mind of man works, does exist in time, does occupy space, and does require energy transformations.

"Admittedly, this is a mystery. How can a non-material attribute such as the mind of man actually influence the organic nervous system? It can be argued that moral law is an example of this kind of thing.

"Moral and spiritual laws do not exist in time, do not occupy space and, so far as anyone knows, no energy transformations, and yet we have evidence, sketchy to be sure, that the so-called spiritual side of existence does influence human behaviour. How this discrepancy between mind and body achieves this, no one knows."

Although Burr understood the nature of the mind, he could not comprehend the influence it had on human behaviour due to the fact that he envisaged the "life fields" as singular rather than plural.

Now that we have ascertained through the research work of Professor Herbert L. König and Dr Walter Kroy that a whole range of fields exist within the aura, our perception of the functioning of those fields have been clarified through the teachings of White Eagle.

White Eagle emphasises the fact we alone are responsible for our own spiritual progress in the following extract: "While on earth you are building your auras, contributing, through your desires to the astral, to the mental and celestial bodies. You are building that celestial body by your actions and reactions, your thoughts and desires."

Constantly, we are reminded that interaction of fields within the aura directly influences our ultimate level of spiritual consciousness, the celestial body.

Thus, because the field of the mind has the power of reasoning through knowledge obtained in the course of day-to-day living, it is possible positively to raise the vibrations of the field to interact and raise the vibrations within the fields of the body elemental and vital bodies. Likewise, negative thoughts within the field of the mind can reduce the vibrations to a level where the field of either the body elemental or the vital body can dominate.

The level of consciousness is reflected in the astral body, which determines, by reason of the law of "like attracts like," the level at which the celestial field functions, which White Eagle refers to as "building the celestial body." This is also the level of consciousness and awareness we shall automatically attain on transition of the individual soul.

The celestial field, functioning on the highest frequency/ vibration within the aura, represents the source of positive thought for the welfare of the individual or the universe at large. Through raising our vibrations within the field of the mind, we can endeavour to attune to that of the celestial field.

White Eagle endeavours to convey this aspect of the aura in his opening words on the subject, "We would now speak of the human aura, remembering that it is only through the medium of the aura that those in spirit are able to communicate with you."

The celestial field, "interpenetrating this (the field of the mind) to a fine degree," registers first as our conscience, but as we develop our consciousness, it becomes God, Allah, The Father, Jesus, Guardian Angel, or simply a guide, according to our conception of the relationship existing between our physical world and the unseen world of spirit.

Viewing our position in the Cosmos from a physical level of frequency/vibrations, if we accept God, Allah, The Father and Jesus (God incarnate) as the Architect of the Universe, then it would be presumptuous of us to assume we have his personal ear.

It makes far more sense to accept the teachings of Silver Birch that as you progress spiritually, you gradually slough off the exterior bodies of your auric field, but maintain contact with an intelligent field which equates to the field of the celestial body in your present aura. In other words, it means that irrespective of your level of consciousness, you have always a being at a higher level of consciousness (frequency/ vibrations) who, by raising the level of vibrations of the individual mind, can impart wisdom and knowledge to assist the individual on his eternal journey.

We can appreciate this steady progression of spirit from our present level of development where, through attuning the field of our mind to that of the celestial field, communication with spirit is attained. Silver Birch describes communication in the following passages:

"When you receive inspiration, it is because consciously or unconsciously you are tuned in to some intelligence within our world and for that time you are able to receive his power, inspiration or message. Sometimes it is conscious; sometimes it is unconscious. It depends on the circumstances...

"But in our life we are constantly receiving and transmitting thoughts. Those who are on our spiritual wavelength, that is, of like spiritual mentality, receive thoughts we transmit to them and they transmit thoughts to us. The wavelength is determined by spiritual attainment.

"You are receiving and transmitting stations. It is very seldom that you construct your own thoughts. Your radio and television have channels, vibrations — frequencies is the right word — to which they can be attuned.

"So you have your frequency. That enables you to receive thoughts, ideas, suggestions, inspiration, guidance and a variety of ideas from those on your wavelengths. As you receive them they are tinctured with your individuality and sent on their way so that others capture them."

In other forms of phenomena, such as psychometry, dowsing, mind-over-matter, etc, the field of the mind is attuned to that of the field of the object matter. The field of the object matter exists because "Matter only exists because of spirit."

Thus, "everything that exists vibrates, radiates and is active." This field exists at a rate of vibration appropriate to the object matter's rating in the animal, vegetable or mineral kingdom, and is capable of retaining and transmit information in a similar manner to the human aura.

As Silver Birch comments: "The ability to tune in to different vibrations depends upon the sensitiveness of the instrument. You are restricted to the vibrations of matter: that is all you can register. The medium who is clairvoyant is able to register finer vibrations of light; the medium who hears registers finer and more subtle vibrations of sound. It depends on the range of the instrument."

Through the fields of the aura, the incarnate spirit has developed his own unique character, and at the same time, prepared a place for himself on the next stage of his eternal journey. His own free will has allowed him to choose his own heaven — or hell! The choice has always been available.

Chapter five

The transition

THE following passages of the teachings of Silver Birch, relating to the life span of mankind is, in my estimation, most apt for it focuses the mind on the continuity of life throughout the universe:

"Think of the miracle of the seasons, the eternal circle forever revolving with unbroken constancy: the snows of winter, when all life sleeps; the herald of spring, when life awakens; the fullness of summer, when life is revealed in all its beauty; autumn, when the voice of nature is hushed and preparation is made for sleep ere the period of refreshment comes upon it.

"The cycle is repeated in every human life. The pageant of nature is duplicated in every human soul. First, there is the spring, with the awakening consciousness; the summer, when man's powers rise to their highest; autumn, when life begins to wane; and winter, when sleep comes to the weary, tired soul.

"But even after the winter of the physical life, spring comes to the spirit as it awakens in another world to continue that eternal cycle. Take from nature this message, and be assured that the laws which have never failed will continue to operate in your case and in the case of every human life."

When we arrive at the "winter of our lives," we are faced with the inevitable. "There is a body of matter, the body of spirit and the vital cord or life-line between them. As disease, infirmity or age creep over the body of matter, there is a gradual loosening in the adjustment between the two bodies because the severance from the world of matter is gradually being accomplished. There are three causes of disease — physical, mental and spiritual."

This is when the spirit is about to return whence it came, and to which Silver Birch refers to in the following terms: "Physical death is equivalent to physical birth. One is the exit of the spirit, the other is its entrance."

In both cases it is the parting of a cord that symbolises the arrival of the soul in both levels of vibration. The parting of the astral cord is the rebirth of the soul into "The Kingdom of heaven," and is no doubt the more logical interpretation placed upon the quotation, "Unless ye be born again, ye cannot enter the Kingdom of heaven."

The continuing growth of nails and hair on the departure of the spirit from the physical body would seem to indicate that the vital field persists for a period after clinical death.

Speaking of the vital body, White Eagle enlightens us as follows: "This departs with the death of the physical body except for a small part that is drawn up into the highest aura, which we will call the celestial aura. The reason for this is that through its contact with earth it has absorbed certain lessons, which are retained to be used in future states of life, not necessarily in the heaven world, but in future incarnations."

This, then, is the casting off of the body we are first aware of, the process which Silver Birch describes as follows: "It is the sloughing off of the physical body as the spirit body gradually emerges. It is never a painful process. There may be some physical reactions when there is illness or disease.

"If the transition is not a simple one, then the equivalent of your doctors stand by. They help those who love this individual to accomplish his or her birth into our world until the cord connecting spirit and matter severs itself and separation is assured for all time.

"The question of awakening is the next to be considered. This depends on the degree of awareness that the newcomer possesses. If completely ignorant of the fact that life continues after earthly death, or if so indoctrinated with false ideas that understanding will take a long time, then there is a process of rest equivalent to sleep.

"That continues until it is self-determined that the time for realisation has come. This can be short or long, as measured by your duration of time. It depends on the individual. Those with knowledge have no such problems. They step out of the world of matter into the world of spirit and adjustment is speedy. When the awakening comes it is a moment of supreme joy because it brings recognition of all the loved ones who have been waiting for it to occur.

"Tears for your world as they pass beyond your ken; rejoicing in ours as we greet newly-liberated souls who will begin to taste the joys of life indescribable in earthly language...

"Do not grieve for those to whom freedom has come. Do not mourn because the caterpillar has become a beauteous butterfly. Do not weep because the cage has been opened and the bird has been set free. Rejoice, and know that the enfranchised soul has found liberty and that, if you would but unfold the powers that the Great Spirit has given you, you could share some of the new beauty and joy which is theirs.

"You could understand the plan of death and realise that death is but a stepping stone, a door through which you enter into the larger realms of spirit...

"If the eyes were open, if the ears could hear, if the soul left behind could register the more subtle vibrations of spiritual life, it would see the resurrected spirit, liberated, triumphant, joyous, welcoming the escape from the thraldom and bondage of a material prison."

Although there has not been what one would term a purely scientific research programme into the transition of the soul, there are those in the medical profession who have sufficient interest in the subject to investigate and detail information provided by several hundred patients who have related their near-death experiences.

Based on the clinical death of the physical body, the reports detail the thoughts and experiences retained in the mind of that particular body during the period of "death." These experiences are of an out-of-the-body type, identical with normal astral travel, but at a greatly extended range.

A brief synopsis which embodies all the common elements of these reports, the order in which the events occur and the manner in which the astral body continues to function outside the confines of the physical body, runs as follows.

A person ceases to breathe and hears the doctor pronounce them "dead." At that moment they begin to hear a loud ringing or buzzing and at the same time experience the sensation of passing rapidly through a long, dark tunnel. Suddenly, they find themselves outside their own physical body, but in the immediate vicinity of the environment in which it can be observed at a distance. From this point of vantage, the attempts at resuscitation of the physical body by medical staff can be witnessed.

Although in a state of emotional upheaval at the time, the mind of the person gradually becomes accustomed to this situation and perceives that they possess a "body," but one very different in nature with that of the physical body left in the hands of the medical staff.

One person described the astral body in the following terms: "I was still in a body, not a physical body, but something I can best describe as an energy pattern. Yet it definitely had different parts."

Spirits of relatives and friends who have already been classified as "dead" come to greet them. A light, at first dim but gradually increasing in power to a brilliance beyond our earthly experience, which, strangely enough, does not appear to unduly affect the astral eyes, draws near.

There is an irresistible magnetic attraction towards this light, which gives off warmth and love of a personal nature towards the spirit suspended between "life" and "death." Irrespective of religious inclination, this "being of light" was regarded as an "emissary, or guide."

Communication between this being and the suspended spirit of the person in the hands of the medical team is carried out by an unimpeded transfer of thought in such a clear manner that there can be no doubting the content of the thoughts, even though they do not appear to be in the native tongue of the person concerned.

The non-verbal thought pattern directed towards the

spirit by this "being of light" is done so in a manner which does not accuse or threaten them. The initial questions are usually in terms of whether one is prepared for death and what has been accomplished in the course of the life one has spent on the earth plane. At all times, the "being of light" exudes overwhelming love, acceptance, understanding and compassion, and is merely there to direct the mind of the suspended spirit into channels that will improve its spiritual progress.

One person described the experience of being in the presence of this entity as "from the moment the light spoke to me, I felt really good — secure and loved. The love that came from it is just unimaginable, indescribable. It was a fun person to be with! And it had a sense of humour, too, definitely!"

Although it is apparent that the "being of light" is aware that the whole of the life of the individual is an open book to him, there is an instant play-back of the complete life span of the suspended spirit. This the spirit reviews and absorbs in detail within a very short time. This exercise appears to be for the "being of light" to impress on the spirit to "love others and acquire knowledge."

There comes a time when either the "being of light" advises the spirit to return to its physical body to continue its earthly span or a barrier of a physical appearance — such as a fence, water or door — separates the earthly life from the spiritual.

On the other side or the barrier are departed relatives and friends of the spirit whom they greet, but advise the spirit that it is not yet time to join them, and must return to complete his or her span upon the earth plane.

Many of the returning spirits felt so comfortable and secure in their disembodied existence that they had no desire to return to the physical world until it came to mind that they still had commitments and responsibilities to those upon the earth plane.

Most individuals say they do not know why or how they returned to their bodies, although they seem to think it was their own decision. However, there are a few more detailed accounts as follows:

"I felt as though I had been called back, magnetised back

through the love of my sister and her husband." Another recalls, "As I was being sucked back, it seemed that the suction started from the head, like I went into the head."

This last quote is a very interesting observation as it tends to corroborate the information provided by Muldoon to the effect that the astral body is attached to the physical body in the area of the medulla oblongata.

The description of the out-of-body experiences of those who volunteered their near-death experiences, which included the attempts made to resuscitate the physical body, comments made by the medical staff and friends, and the many positions from which the physical body was viewed, substantiates the fact that the whole of the faculties of the physical body are contained within the astral body, with the added faculty of communication by thought transference.

The teachings of these "beings of light," quoted by persons of mixed religious beliefs, are identical to those of Silver Birch. It will be noted that once again emphasis is placed on the acquisition of knowledge and the need to love others in order to progress spiritually.

A particular remark addressed to the suspended spirit of one individual by his "guardian angel" is worthy of quoting, "I have helped you through this stage of your existence, but now I am going to turn you over to others."

This illustrates the relationship existing between the field of the mind and that of the celestial, as previously discussed, where "like attracts like." As the field of the mind develops its consciousness, it attracts an entity ("guardian angel") of an appropriate level into the celestial field of the individual.

Reference to "energy patterns," "magnetic attraction" and "magnetised back" is not a mere coincidence, but indicates the relationship between the experiences of these individuals and the results obtained in the course of scientific research into the electromagnetic nature of the aura. For lay persons to use such terminology is rather unusual by any standards.

When one contemplates the teachings of the philosopher Plato on the subject of life and death, one will realise that we are only now getting back to his original concept of the universe and the manner in which mankind relates to it. Apart from using logic and reason in his discussions in search of truth, he was also a visionary, one who considered that truth could ultimately only come from an experience of a spiritual nature, providing an insight into the mysteries of the universe.

Plato was also aware of the existence of other planes of reality apart from the physical world in which he lived, and believed that it was only through contact with these sources that we could understand the true nature of our own world.

In birth, it is the descent of the spirit or soul from these higher and more divine planes into a physical body, where it registers at a lower level of awareness to that prevailing in its previous plane of existence. He recognised the physical body as being but a temporary vehicle of the soul.

Death is merely the departure of the soul from the physical body, which, on its journey back to those higher planes of existence, meets and speaks with the departed spirits of others who have gone before and is guided through the whole of the transition by guardian spirits.

Plato refers to the physical body as the prison of the soul, and speaks of the sense of freedom experienced on release from the physical body, and the fact that it is far easier to think and reason more clearly in recognising the true nature of the universe.

How is it, then, that this truth, known four hundred years before the birth of Christ, did not prevail?. The answer lies in Silver Birch's indictment of the part played by religion throughout history:

"Your churches have divided mankind, separated nations and classes, caused wars and bitterness, rancour, bloodshed, torture, inquisition. They have opposed the march of knowledge, invention, science, discovery. They have sought to protect a vested interest, fearful and afraid lest the new knowledge should engulf them. The truth is here to stay. It cannot be stemmed any longer."

We all come from the same source to which we return so there should be no question of division amongst us, as Silver Birch teaches:

"Ours is but the simple truth which in its utter simplicity

can be appreciated and understood by all for we strive to reveal the Children of the Great Spirit as they are — part of the Great Spirit, truly the children of God, all bound together by the infinite eternal tie of spirit, all part of a vast spiritual family, all equal in the sight of the Great Spirit.

"Those who see with the eyes of the spirit see beyond the confines of barriers of race, nationality, clime, colour and creed and discern that tie of the spirit that binds together all humanity as one.

"It is very necessary to remind your world of these simple truths. For too long have they floundered in creeds and dogmas, ceremonies and rituals which have nothing whatever to do with religion or the Great Spirit of life"

We are "all part of a vast spiritual family, all equal in the sight of the Great Spirit," echoes the teaching of Paul in 1 Corinthians 12-13. "For by one Spirit are we all baptised into one body, whether we be Jews or Gentiles, whether we be bond or free; and have been all made to drink into one Spirit." This rather unfortunate habit of the teachers of that period speaking in oblique terms has lead to many misinterpretations of the content of the teaching.

The worst example of this misinterpretation occurs in 1 Corinthians, Chapter 15, where Paul is attempting to explain the transition. His teaching is correct, but the terminology used has had a rather unfortunate impact on fundamental Christians. There is no doubt, however, with regard to his statement that the physical body "is sown a natural body (conception), is raised a spiritual body (the arrival of the incarnating spirit at birth)."

Paul tends to vary his terms of reference in his description of the change experienced at "death." Therefore, if we replace corruption and corruptible with physical body and incorruption and incorruptible with spiritual body, perhaps we can more easily comprehend his teaching. 1 Corinthians, 15 — 51 tells us quite clearly that "we shall not sleep, but we shall all be changed." One cannot interpret that extract in any other way than in "death" we shall retain our sense of awareness, although in a different form.

It is 1 Corinthians, 15 — 52 which has been the cause of much controversy, and, no doubt, misery to those who have misconstrued his words: "In a moment, in a twinkling of an eye, at the last trump; for the trumpet shall sound, and the dead shall be raised (a) spiritual body and we shall be changed."

It is unfortunate that Paul used the term "trumpet." In interpreting this passage, I would suggest that the trumpet call he alluded to was the one used when fighting men were called upon to retire or retreat. Equating this suggestion with the passage, in modern idiom this should read, "at death, for death is a certainty."

The idea of one remaining in a state of "death" awaiting a trumpet call in order physically to resurrect is biologically unsound and capable of causing historical chaos. The mind runs riot when one reflects on a buried body, the worms, the birds of the air and those that feed off them.

With cremation, there is a larger problem, if that is possible, in imagining how physical resurrection can take place. Think also of the billions of persons who have during the course of their lives upon earth embraced Christianity over the centuries. Earth would not hold them.

What really is the point of physical resurrection when Paul, in the same chapter, teaches that "flesh and blood cannot inherit the Kingdom of God"? Jesus, in John 23 - 43 does not request the thief on the cross to await the call of the trumpet prior to resurrection, "Verily I say unto thee, today shalt thou be with me in paradise."

We cannot therefore be surprised that Silver Birch refers to these maligned teachings of the resurrection with regard to the awakening of the spirit at transition in the following terms: "This depends on the degree of awareness that the newcomer possesses. If completely ignorant of the fact that life continues after earthly death or if so indoctrinated with false ideas that understanding will take a long time, then there is a process of rest equivalent to sleep.

"That continues until it is self-determined that the time for realisation has come. This can be short or long, as measured by your duration or time. It depends on the individual.

"Those with knowledge have no such problems. They step out of the world of matter into the world of spirit and adjustment is speedy. When awakening comes it is a moment of supreme joy because it brings recognition of all the loved ones who have been waiting for it to occur."

Paul taught the truth that "we shall not sleep" at the moment of death. It is rather difficult to understand how so many people have been convinced contrary to this teaching. This illustrates the fact that knowledge must always supersede faith in the words of others.

Each individual must continuously search for fresh knowledge that appeals to his common sense, rejecting all that repels it. Always bear in mind that truth is relevant to the level of consciousness attained. Therefore, what may represent truth to one person may not necessarily appear to be true to another individual.

Chapter six

The planes of vibration

TO comprehend the nature of the world of spirit, which we shall, in time, inherit, we must bear in mind the words of Silver Birch: "You are as much in the next world as ever you will be. It is only a question of your rate of vibration...Death will not transform you into a spiritual being; death will not enhance your spiritual stature by one iota.

"You are spirit here and now. The rate of vibration of the astral body, at this particular level of physical vibration, determines the level of the vibration of the plane of existence you will automatically be attracted to on transition.

"The manner in which you have lived your span of life upon the earth plane and the level of consciousness you have developed determine the level of vibration upon which your present astral body functions. This principle also applies in the higher planes of vibration of which we become aware on transition."

Silver Birch refers to these planes, existing at differing levels of vibration, in the following terms: "It is an intermingling. It is like the vibrations of the wireless which fill all space; there are different wavelengths, different vibrations, but they are all occupying the same space at the same time...

"There is no boundary, there is no frontier...They are registering different vibrations; they are functioning on a different plane or aspect of consciousness."

Service to others is the key to raising the vibrations of the controlling body, which functions as the astral body at the level of vibration which the spirit mind operates in order to progress to the next stage of evolution. Silver Birch enlightens us a little further on the mode of progress in these planes of vibration:

"In our life you occupy just that sphere to which you have grown, that is, the sphere with which you harmonise because your mental, moral and spiritual growth determine it. The difference is purely the difference of the people who live it.

"The higher you are spiritually, the better you are. The kinder you are, the more charitable you are, the more unselfish you are, the higher is the level on which you live in your world."

Once the levels of vibration begin to rise in the controlling body, the apparent physical body gradually begins to fade until it disappears, and the next stage in evolution is attained. In this manner, as the consciousness develops through harmony within the mind, one draws nearer to the Great Spirit.

That, briefly, is the basis of the manner in which these vibrating planes of existence relate to each other. As Silver Birch informs us, they are "Far more real and far more solid than the one that you leave behind in the world of matter." To provide more detail of life experienced in the various planes, which is obviously the "sorting of the wheat from the chaff," we will return to the teachings of Silver Birch

At all times during our life-span upon the earth plane, "You are subject to the whole range of spirit influence from the lowest to the highest. But you attract only those at the spiritual stage you have reached. Evil can be attracted by evil. Saintliness always attracts saintliness. That is how the natural law operates."

Thus, according to the thoughts generated within the mind of the individual and the lifestyle adopted, depends the type of environment which will be enjoyed on arrival in the new plane of existence on transition. Silver Birch refers to the problems of the misguided spirits who inhabit cemeteries waiting for their Judgement Day thus:

"They expect these things. Nothing can be done with

them until they learn to change their thoughts. For practically all their earthly lives they have moulded the thought form that, when the body dies, they will wait until the Angel Gabriel sounds his trumpet. And until they can destroy, with adjustment, the power that they have created, it holds them in that prison...

"It is just the same as those who refuse to believe it (that they are dead). We cannot make them believe it. You have no idea of the difficulties when we try to convince them that they are dead."

The question of the retention of the normal functions of life in the astral world elicited this response: "Whether they retain these organs depends on their stage of consciousness. If they are completely ignorant of a life after yours, and do not think that there is another world, then they have a complete replica of everything they had in the physical world, and continue every bodily function in all its details.

"Of course, it is possible to sin in our world. The sins of the spirit world are the sins of selfishness, but in our world they are speedily revealed. They are known as soon as the thought is in the mind. The effect is seen far more quickly than it is in your world of matter.

"It registers on the one who commits the sin and makes him spiritually lower than he was before. It is difficult to define more clearly in your language what these sins are, except that they are sins of selfishness."

For those aware of the world of spirit, Silver Birch enlightens us further: "The astral body goes through a process of rarefication (change to a higher vibration). As you appreciate that there is no need for certain organs, you gradually find they become atrophied and in the end they disappear." When asked if this was a gradual process or otherwise, Silver Birch replied:

"It depends on the state of your consciousness. The higher the consciousness, the less need for adjustment. You must always remember that ours is a mind world (a world existing at the level of vibration of the mind) a spirit world where consciousness is king...

"The lower planes, the astral ones, are in many respects a duplicate of earthly existence. This is a divine provision to enable newly-arrived inhabitants to acclimatise themselves, otherwise it would be too difficult for them."

At this period of developing consciousness, we have arrived at the stage, when, as Jesus taught, "And shall come forth; they that have done good unto the resurrection of life; and they that have done evil, into the resurrection of damnation."

This is reinforced by the words within the "Bhagavad Gita" "For those who worship the gods go to the gods and those who worship the fathers go to the fathers. Those who worship the lower spirits go to the lower spirits; but those that worship me come to me."

It is therefore obvious that resurrection of the soul has always been within the teachings of the prophets. Unfortunately, the followers of the prophets have not interpreted the teachings in the correct manner. Perhaps the message was too simple: live in harmony, serve others, and develop your consciousness.

Questioned as to whether one's spirit life commenced in the lower astral planes, Silver Birch replied: "Oh, no, it is for the uninstructed and ignorant, those who are unaware of the existence of spiritual realities, who cannot visualise anything beyond the purely physical. The astral world is part of the world of spirit. It is one life in many varying grades, from the lower reaches to the highest stages.

"Spirit life is graduated, with each sphere, plane or expression, blending and shading into the next one higher in the evolutionary sense but not in geographical location. As the soul progresses and fits itself for higher states of being so automatically it occupies those states...

"The lower gives way to the higher. You 'die' and are born again. You do not lose the astral body in quite the same way that you lose the material body. It becomes more rarefied (raising of the vibrations). It becomes refined as the lower drops away. That is its death for death really means transformation, resurrection, the rising of the higher out of the lower...

"The more you evolve, the more of the unexpressed self comes to the surface. That means more of perfection is being expressed the closer you are to the Great Spirit. If perfection was a finite process, then you would, in a stated time, merge with the Great Spirit, but it is an infinite process for the more you evolve, the more you realise there is to be evolved so that you are becoming more and more individualised as time goes by."

Having completed a quick survey of the manner in which spiritual progress is related to the level of vibrations produced by the mind at any stage of conscious awareness, and the automatic attraction (of an electromagnetic nature) to a higher plane of vibration as the level of vibration within the field of the mind increases, we can now accept it is the "seed atom" that has an eternal existence through its many stages of evolution.

One may also assume that evolution is of the mind, not the physical body, for all form we observe is moulded and maintained by the vital field pattern surrounding it.

We may also recognise the fact that there is a law which is obedient to the level of consciousness of the mind, and cannot be manipulated. One must therefore realise that spiritual progress may only be attained through the complete thought process of the mind related to one's activities.

Obviously, within the lower planes exist a broader band of vibrations of individual minds, similar to that we experience in this world. The higher the plane of existence, the narrower becomes the band of vibration; the closer we come to that of light, which provides an answer to the soul or mind, being greeted by a "being of light" from the higher realms. In reply to the question, "Does colour form the basis of recognition when you get beyond shape?" Silver Birch replied:

"Yes, but whereas you are governed by certain primary colours we have other ranges of colour beyond your comprehension. We can identify some of the higher teachers by their appearance, by the light that comes with the message because often there is no form of any kind. There is a thought accompanied by radiance.

"Within the lower vibrations of the astral world, we have those souls who are unaware that they are no longer in the physical world and exist in limbo." As Silver Birch explains: "You must remember that there is no such thing as time to us. If they knew they were waiting that would destroy the thought form. It is a self-made prison."

This is the plane of vibrations in which those who are ignorant of the after-life dwell, many of whom have been dispatched from the physical world in a precipitate manner, either in battle or other violent means. The reaction in the field of the mind is such that they cannot progress mentally, and therefore spiritually, and remain tied to those last moments experienced on the earth plane. Time has stood still for them. They continue to replay those last moments, which we observe as "hauntings."

These unfortunates have lost all contact with their celestial field, and consequently with those who guide them, either through fear and terror, or the constant erroneous brain-washing of the field of the mind whilst on the earth-plane. Silver Birch describes this latter group as, "Those that are ignorant, those who are prejudiced, those who allow their lives to be ordered by superstition, provide mental barriers, each of which is an obstacle to the power of the spirit, and the nature of the obstacle determines the time it takes to break it down."

This group is at least on a level of vibration where, through mediumship, they may be acquainted with the fact that they no longer inhabit the earth-plane, and advised on the manner in which they can progress towards the "beings of light."

Even further away from the "beings of light," in terms of planes of vibration, are those which have, throughout their life-span on earth, brought about total disharmony by committing acts of violence, robbery, sexual indulgence, drink and drugs.

On the lowest planes of vibration exist those entities who have debased, debauched, tortured and butchered innocent members of the human race. From time to time, throughout the history of man, these entities have appeared upon the earth-plane to wreak their havoc.

The greatest excesses inflicted on humanity occurred during the period of the Inquisition, when the Roman Catholic Church was in the process of "converting" non-believers to the faith with sword and cross, and again when sub-humans eliminated millions of human beings of the Jewish faith in the death camps of Europe during World War 2 .

Today, we still have those upon the earth-plane who have no regard for human life or values. Unfortunately, many of the individuals who come within this classification are also accepted as being representative of their particular brand of religion.

One would consider that religion consisted of the teaching of love and harmony to all men in the light of their particular prophet, not the decrees laid down by their followers in order to manipulate the masses. These individuals not only reduce their own level of vibration of the astral body by their actions and words, but also influence the minds of others with a similar result.

At transition, because "like attracts like," these entities find themselves automatically drawn to the lower planes of existence where those of a similar nature who have gone before wait to greet them. There they will join their "friends" in the appropriate environment and spend their discarnate life wallowing in crime or debauchery, according to the level of vibration of the mind and, therefore, the astral body.

These entities have forfeited further spiritual progress because they have reduced their mental vibrations to a level that the "beings of light" are unable to contact them. However, there are individuals on the earth-plane with minds akin to that of the astral planes and others who lack will power. Such people allow these entities to control their minds and bodies in order once more to experience the physical world.

Thus evil is perpetuated from a "hell" created by man, who, through misuse of his free will, has caused within the universe planes of vibration of disharmony. These are in direct opposition to the universal law of harmony.

This is self-explanatory for man is the only creature on earth to have sufficient intelligence and know-how to indulge in devious and violent practices. The remainder of the Great Spirit's creatures only possess a mind that is merely capable of procreation and seeking food.

Silver Birch refers to the matter of free will as follows: "In that sense, you might argue that the Great Spirit is responsible for those who are depraved, for those who are unenlightened that they render harm to their brothers in your world. But to each one of you is given the amount of free will which, as you evolve, you learn to exercise. The higher you evolve in the spiritual scale, the greater can you exercise your free will."

Jesus in Matthew 10:28 also refers to the relationship between the soul and "hell" by saying, "And fear not them which kill the body, but are not able to kill the soul, but rather fear him which is able to destroy both soul and body in hell."

Paul, in Romans 8:6 also speaks of the consequences which are dependent on the level of consciousness of the mind: "For to be carnally minded is death; but to be spiritually minded is life and peace." "Kill" and "death," when related to the soul/mind in these passages, means that spiritual progress is no longer possible, as I have previously indicated.

The "Bhagavad Gita" of the Hindus also refers to those who of their own choice have rejected spiritual progress: "In the vast cycles of life and death I inexorably hurl them down to destruction; these the lowest of men, cruel and evil, whose soul is hate. Reborn in a lower life, in darkness after birth they come not to me, Arjuna; but they go down the path of hell. Three are the gates to this hell and the death of the soul; the gate of lust, the gate of wrath, and the gate of greed. Let a man shun the three."

Thus mankind, with its free will, creates its own "heaven" or "hell" upon the earth-plane. Within the higher planes of vibration exist the "many mansions" to which, according to the material processed through the mind during the course of one's life-span, one is automatically attracted to on transition. These are the planes of vibration from which the ordinary man in the street has his first experience of life within the spirit world.

Silver Birch elaborates on the part free will plays in the transition of the soul: "There will always be a struggle in your world between the two forces which seek to control man, his animal ancestry, the force of the brutish beast that belongs to his physical evolution, and the divine spirit, the breath of the Great Spirit, which unites him with the infinite processes of creation.

"Man's free will decides in this constant struggle in your world which will obtain the mastery and succeed in holding it. When you come to our world, there is struggle in the sense that there is a constant effort to overcome faults of the lower nature, to give rise to the higher innate qualities of the spirit; the struggle towards perfection, towards the light; the struggle in which you are discarding all the grosser elements of your being, as, strengthened, purified, refined and tested, the pure gold of the spirit gradually emerges."

The world of spirit into which we shall be welcomed is defined by Silver Birch thus: "The next stage of life to earth is a replica of your world of matter. Were it not so, the shock for the many who are uninstructed and ignorant would be more than they could stand so it has to be accomplished by very easy stages. The next stage of life resembles your world. That is why so many do not know that they have passed beyond the physical.

"Here essentially it is a world of thought, where thought is reality. Being a thought world, thought moulds every expression of its life and its activity. Being so near to your world, and peopled by men and women who are naturally still very material in their outlook on life, the expression of their thought is very gross and so whatever they think is in terms of physical things.

"They cannot think of life apart from its physical aspects. There has never filtered into their consciousness any understanding of a life apart from the purely physical. They cannot visualise spiritual activities. Because they cannot visualise them, they have no place in their scheme of things.

"But there are degrees of astral life for gradually as awakening comes, the grossness slowly disappears and becomes more refined. Life, they begin to see, is something beyond its material aspect. When spiritual realisation dawns, they are dead to the astral world and they begin to live in the world of spirit. There are many deaths and many births."

The "many deaths and many births" refer, of course, to the fact that as one evolves from one plane of vibration to the next, "so automatically you discard the body that has served its purpose and assume the one that is fitted for your stage of evolution."

Silver Birch expands further in describing his world of spirit: "It is very hard for me to convey to you what life in our world is really like. I speak truthfully when I tell you there is much to explore on this side. You have no knowledge of the infinite richness of the life in the world of spirit. There is no beauty anywhere, no majestic scenery, nothing you have visualised that can compare in its grandeur and in its infinite variety to that which can be seen in our world.

"You have no idea of the wonders, beauty, richness, glory and the radiance of life in our world. It is impossible to find language to describe it for you...

"Life in our world is on varying levels of being, not in isolation, but merging into one another. Thus on one plane of being, objective reality, in the term that you use it, is the same for all who are there. They have hills, mountains, rivers, streams, birds, flowers and trees which are real.

"There is nothing in your world of matter with which you can compare the life of spirit, freed from the trammels of the flesh, escaped from the prison of the body of matter, with liberty to go where you will, to see your thoughts take shape, to follow the desires of your heart, to be freed from the troubles of money...

"This is the world where there are no clumsy words to express inspiration, but where thought is the living language and reveals itself with lightning rapidity. This is the world where we have no money to worry us, where there is no competition, no driving of the weaker to the wall, where the strong are strong because they have something to give to those less fortunate than themselves.

"We have no unemployment; we have no slums; we have no selfishness; we have no sects. We have only one religion. We have no sacred books, only the operation of the divine laws to instruct us.

"Do you call it tragic to express yourself in a body that has no pain, to be able to roam all over the world of matter in a flash and to taste the beauties of the spirit life too?

"This is the world where the artist finds all his dreams come true, where the painter and the poet realise their ambition, where genius has full power of expression, where the repressions of earth are swept away and all gifts and talents are used in the service of one another.

"There is not in your world one artist who could capture with his paints some of the glories of my world. There is not one musician who could record some of the glories of the music sphere with your notes. There is not one writer who could describe in physical words the beauty of parts of this world.

"Your world is in beauty now (May). You see all around you the manifestations of the Great Spirit, as the dawn of life sweeps over your surroundings again in its cycle, and you marvel at the beauty of the blossoms and the fragrance of the flowers, and you say, 'How great is the handiwork of the Great Spirit.'

"Yet that which you see is but a very, very pale reflection of the beauties that we have in our world of spirit. We have flowers such as you have never seen; we have colours such as your eye has never beheld; we have scenes and forests; we have birds and plants; we have streams and mountains. You have nothing to compare them with. And you will be able to enjoy them. Even though you will be 'ghosts,' you will be real ones."

This is a brief résumé of the life awaiting those who have lived their earthly lives in a reasonable manner and run their allotted span. This gives the lie to those who pronounce that "No one has ever come back from the dead to tell us what awaits us when we die." There are many taped recordings, especially those recorded through the direct voice mediumship of Leslie Flint, in which discarnate entities describe the particular plane of vibration they occupy.

These speak of hospitals and homes of rest where those who have suffered long periods of hospitalisation on the earth-plane and are unaware of the continuity of life are gradually brought to the realisation of the nature of the new environment they inhabit.

They describe the new homes they occupy, the new interests they are able to indulge in, the beautiful halls and buildings that exist for lectures on the arts and the appreciation of music. Attempts are also made to describe the brilliance of the colours of the worlds in which they live and the added lustre this provides to their surroundings, where the power of thought provides them with every need.

With such a beautiful scenario, there is no fear of death to those who respond to the natural laws of the universe. Once the astral cord has parted from the physical body, there is no more pain. One arrives at one's destination to be greeted by loved ones and continue to be still aware of those remaining on the earth-plane.

To those who find themselves separated from their loved ones by transition, I commend the words of Henry Scott Holland, Canon of St Paul's Cathedral, who passed to the Higher Life in 1918:

"Death is nothing at all. I have only slipped away into the next room. I am I, and you are you. Whatever we were to each other, that we still are. Call me by my old familiar name, speak to me in the easy way you always used. Put no difference in your tone, wear no forced air of solemnity or sorrow. Laugh as we always laughed at the little jokes we enjoyed together. Pray, smile, think of me, pray for me.

"Let my name be ever the household word that it always was. Let it be spoken without effect, without a shadow on it. Life means all that it ever meant. It is the same as it ever was; there is unbroken continuity. Why should I be out of mind because I am out of sight? I am waiting for you, for an interval, somewhere very near, just around the corner. All is well."

Let us conclude with Silver Birch's view of fear of the unknown: "You should always welcome the morrow as the harbinger of a wondrous adventure and possibility that it has for you. Your life should be exhilarating. Cast out fear. Fear is a product of ignorance and superstition. We are privileged to live in the sunlight of knowledge."

Chapter seven

Health and the vibrant aura

IF we are to comprehend fully the manner in which our health is influenced throughout our lives by unseen factors, we must have a better understanding of the part played by the fields — or bodies — of the conscious and subconscious mind, and that of the vital body and body elemental.

The vital field or body — as the pattern or mould of the physical body, engaged in forming and maintaining same — is vibrating at a constant rate at the lower end of the range existing within the aura. The body elemental exists at a slightly higher rate of vibration to that of the vital field and equates with that of the mind level of the animal species.

These two fields are what one may describe as part of the fixed design of the Great Spirit, which functions within very narrow bands of the lower frequencies, or vibrations, of the universal structure. The field of the mind, through its free will, has a broad spectrum of vibrations in which to indulge, but is governed by the negative or positive input received via the five senses of the physical body.

Silver Birch speaks of the relationship between these fields in the following terms:

"The power of the spirit fashioned all life, which controls every motion and mutation of natural force, regulates all the seasons and governs the growth of every seed of every plant, bush and tree, the power that is responsible for the whole scheme of evolution, in all its intricate phases. Wherever life takes conscious form, there you have individual spirit. That is the difference between you and the beasts. Man (the incarnate mind) is an individuated spirit, part of the Great Spirit."

Thus the mind of man is the "divine spark within." which, although at the lower range of vibrations, is nevertheless, part of the Supreme Intelligence which controls and directs the whole of the universe.

In order to take a more active part in bringing the universe into a more harmonious state, we have to realise that the vibrations within the field of the mind must be raised by positive thinking, as expressed by Silver Birch: "Compassion is one of the attributes of the Spirit. I have said it so many times. Love, affection, friendship, compassion, mercy, tolerance, kindness, service, are the attributes of the Spirit. When you express them, you are manifesting yourself spiritually."

Progress through the various planes of vibration is governed by this attitude of mind towards others on the pathway to perfection. Negative thinking, which reduces the vibrations of the mind to that approaching that of the body elemental, is focused on by Silver Birch thus, "You are engaged in a great battle against greed, selfishness, cupidity, stupidity and all the horrible results of materialism that cause trouble."

These expressions of disharmony cover all the major causes of the destruction of the moral fibre of our society, which leads to the automatic attraction of the astral body to the lower vibrations on transition, and provides the spirit world with added complications. Silver Birch refers to this problem, saying:

"Our world is composed of people who come from your world. If you did not send us unevolved souls, we would have no trouble from them. You send millions who are unprepared, unfitted and ignorant. It is much more difficult to teach an adult the lessons he should have learnt in school...Evil can only be attracted by evil."

Therefore, we have the mind, the incarnate spirit, which is capable, by means of the thoughts processed through it by the five physical senses, of rising, in terms of vibrations, to the heights of the field of the aura, or regress down to that of the level of the body elemental.

We have free will. It is up to ourselves which path we pursue. Only through knowledge can one make a responsible decision.

We, at our level of development, are not really aware of the great potential that lies within the mind, but Silver Birch elucidates:

"The human mind possesses great potency, and the constant dwelling upon certain beliefs and circumstances can enable those happenings to be re-enacted on your physical body. Mind is stronger than matter, for matter is but a lower expression of the mind. Mind has moulded matter so that mind can have a channel of expression. Mind is dominant. Mind is king. Mind is ruler.

"Everything that happens in your world affects your body of matter and, in turn, everything that affects your spiritual body (mind) reacts on your physical body. There are forces of action and reaction at work all the time."

When asked "Would an illness caused by infection come through purely physical causes?" Silver Birch replied, "Not necessarily, because there are many diseases that have no real physical causes, but start with the spirit (mind)." In answer to the question, "What causes these diseases?" he replied: "Selfishness, greed, avarice. You know the story of the Nazarene who told the man, 'Your sins are forgiven.'

"You must realise there are both physical and spiritual (mind) causes for your disorders. They could all be treated in the same way, but some are more easily treated in the physical way. Though the etheric body (vital body) is affected by illness and sometimes even causes illness, there is no real illness in the spiritual body (mind).

"It is a defect in its adjustment with the body of matter (via the vital body). It would affect its vibrations and relationship with the body of matter to such an extent that disease would begin in the body of matter. Anger can affect the spleen. Jealousy can affect the liver.

"Those things cause maladjustment. The perfect balance is distorted and the harmony is upset. When the body becomes so diseased that the balance is completely upset, then the body of the spirit (mind/incarnate spirit) is compelled to sever itself because it can no longer express itself through that body and death takes place."

When asked how the loss of a physical arm affected the etheric body (vital body), Silver Birch replied: "There is nothing that would happen to the etheric body (vital body), but there would be a lack of adjustment between the two arms. The etheric (vital) arm could not function while you were in the body of matter."

It will be noted from this last passage that the loss of a physical limb does not detract from the etheric, or vital body, which remains intact. This compliments the conclusion reached by Kirlian that the removal of a section of leaf by cutting left the auric field intact.

"Lack of adjustment between the two arms" occurs because although the mould that forms and maintains the physical body is still intact, it no longer has that particular area of the physical body (the arm) to service. If medical science provides the material, I have no doubt that new limbs, given time and patience, can be reproduced.

One can understand from these passages the part played by the mind and vital fields of the aura through constant "action and reaction." Because of their electromagnetic nature, there is an automatic response to a change of vibration in one field, producing a similar change in the other.

If the level of vibrations are raised in the field of the mind by positive thinking, automatically, by interaction, the vibrations within the vital body are raised and the condition of the physical body is improved.

Negative thoughts within the field of the mind, whether conscious or sub-conscious, reduce the level of vibrations within the vital field and bring about a deterioration of the health of the physical body. Conversely, the condition of the physical body can negatively bias the field of the mind via the vital body.

Many "hereditary" diseases, I would suggest, stem from the sub-conscious mind of members of a particular family or group, whose forebears have departed this life with certain conditions. The obvious way to overcome this problem is to develop a more positive attitude within the conscious mind in order to displace the negative vibrations within the vital field.

Ill-health therefore appears to stem from the sub-conscious area of the field of the mind. One can begin to comprehend the manner in which the visualisation technique functions.

In accepting the manner in which the conscious mind interacts electromagnetically with that of the sub-conscious, and in turn, the vital field controlling the physical body, one becomes aware that through positive visualisation of a negative medical condition within the physical body, restoration to its normal healthy state can be accomplished. This is the fundamental basis of all visualisation techniques, irrespective of the symbolic or natural nature of the picture used for the healing process.

This method of self-healing has been employed with success in many cases. Once the link between the mind, conscious and sub-conscious with the vital controlling field of the physical body is accepted, we should observe a general improvement in the health of the people through fresh techniques employed by the medical profession.

In spiritual healing, it is the conscious mind field of the healer — strengthened by the interaction of the field of those of a higher level of consciousness, functioning within the celestial range of vibrations — that interacts in a similar manner with the sub-conscious or vital fields of the patient. Because the field of the conscious mind can be instructed and directed by those competent in the application, absent healing may be accomplished since the mind, as demonstrated in recall of astral travel, is not limited by time or distance.

Flooding the conscious/sub-conscious fields of the mind with healing thoughts through the use of suitably worded cassette tapes, will, no doubt become part of our normal medical treatment.

By positive thoughts and action, we can avoid many of the health hazards that beset us throughout our lives, which emphasises the old adage, "A healthy mind in a healthy body." Providing the patient has a normal appetite, there is no necessity for special diets. All healing can be accomplished through the fields of the sub-conscious and vital bodies. Food is merely the means of providing material matter for the vital body to manipulate.

One method of healing which has been sadly neglected

is hypnosis. If we accept that by influencing the sub-conscious area of the mind we can control the condition of the physical body via the interaction of the field of the mind with that of the vital field, hypnosis can be the answer to many medical problems. The main factor in healing is to instill into the patients' sub-conscious mind the conviction they will be restored to full health and vigour.

The tool for removing all negative thoughts from the sub-conscious area of the patient's mind and replacing them with positive healing thoughts is hypnosis.

If we consider the variety of ailments that have been treated successfully by hypnosis, it becomes obvious that far from being an alternative therapy, as the medical profession would have us believe, it is the natural method of healing without resorting to drugs. The following list of successful hypnotic treatments carried out by Ralph Slater, an authority on this method of treatment, gives some idea of the scope of this medium:

The treatment of eczema and other skin disorders.

Rectifying conditions affecting, heart, liver, pancreas and lungs.

The treatment of nervous and mental conditions.

Relief of pain of migraine, headache, neuralgia and rheumatism.

Correction of habits such as smoking, drinking, insomnia, phobias and other neurotic disorders.

Pre and post operation suggestions to reduce pain and improve the rate of healing.

A cripple walking with a stick, who had to be helped up the stairs by others, left the stage walking steadily and proudly under his own steam.

An old man shaking all over with some functional nervous disorder, who was regarded by himself and others to be unemployable and had drawn war disability pension for years, stood up straight and strong again like the fine young soldier he had been.

Perhaps it has been the fact that the medical profession have never understood the manner in which the mind controls the physical welfare of the body that has made them wary of using this particular medium. Any qualified medical practitioner, using hypnosis under regulated conditions, should be capable of producing quicker recovery times, with a higher success rate, without side effects.

When asked, "Is hypnotism a good subject for study?" Silver Birch replied: "If the man who hypnotises is of good intent, and the desire to use his power for service, then, of course it is good. The hypnotist is only tapping some of the latent powers of the soul...

"If the hypnotist is of good intent, he can perform great service for he can stimulate the divine within. But he can also stimulate the animal within."

The advantage of hypnosis over the visualisation technique lies in the suggestions or instructions of the operator being directed to the subconscious area of the mind without intervention from the conscious mind of the subject. With the conscious mind in a state of inactivity, suspension or withdrawal, the instructions given to the sub-conscious mind are obeyed without question.

The only exception to this broad statement is, generally speaking, that the subject will not accept any suggestions he is opposed to moral or religious principles. However, I am not convinced that this can be taken for granted. It is up to the operator and subject to ensure that the operation is conducted under regulated conditions.

If we accept the conclusions of Ralph Slater that "The operator does not hypnotise the subject, the subject hypnotises himself," it becomes obvious that the natural sleep state is attained by self-hypnosis.

I have been made aware of this fact by unsolicited experiments carried out by a friend of mine during my war service. There is, therefore, a relationship between hypnosis, self-hypnosis, sleep and trance mediumship.

The development of trance mediumship, like hypnosis, is attained virtually by self-hypnosis and the co-operation, with, in one case, the entrancing entity, and in the other, the operator. In either case, the conscious mind is placed in a state of inaction or withdrawal while the subconscious continues to function normally.

With the conscious mind, which normally reacts to the five senses of the physical body, inactive, these same faculties respond to the spoken word of the operator, or indeed, the thoughts projected by those from another vibration, impinging upon the sub-conscious. This can, in the course of hypnosis, result in rather bizarre effects being produced in which the subject reacts in a totally different — and even opposite — manner to that which would appertain when under the control of the conscious mind.

An example of this behaviour pattern is through hypnotic suggestion. An individual given an empty tumbler can be made to react in such a manner that one would assume he or she had consumed a glass of whisky.

As it is an established fact that the hypnotist can pass control of a subject to another person or entity, it would appear that the hypnotist could play a prominent part, in conjunction with a clairvoyant, in the development of trance mediumship.

Silver Birch has a few words to say on the subject of hypnotism as an aid to trance mediumship:

"It has been tried, but it has been found that once the guides take charge, the power of the hypnotist in your world is at an end for the medium does not then come within the range of his influence.

"It is not advisable because once a medium has become subject to spirit power he is outside the influence of the hypnotist. It would be better for him to start his development in seances so that the spirit power can begin gradually to exert its influence over him."

Summing up, we can conclude that we are a product of the mind and "As we think, so we are." Therefore, it behoves us constantly, by a mild form of self-hypnosis, to pass from the conscious mind into the sub-conscious constructive thoughts. In this manner one can maintain a fit, healthy body or even bring about conditions in life which one desires.

To increase the effectiveness of self-hypnosis, it is suggested that ten to fifteen minutes, upon retiring and awakening, be devoted to think or speak the instructions you wish to deposit within the sub-conscious. By this means, one can anticipate a long and healthy life.

Chapter eight

"Spirit" and evolution

LET us open this chapter with the words of Silver Birch: "Before you learn, you must unlearn. You must discard all that which hinders your minds from thinking as they should. Thus your soul and spirit grow and you are ready for higher knowledge.

"You learn natural law through the evolution of your own spirit. You learn first of all to discard all that which is false, all that which makes your reason revolt...

"That is why we emphasise the laws of the Great Spirit for the true understanding of these laws harmonises all knowledge...Your world needs this knowledge because it will illuminate the whole of life, and make what was incomprehensible easy to understand.

"It will enable men to cease to be tortured by all the crudities and inadequacies of erroneous teachings that have for too long acted as a brake on progress...You become free when you are not afraid to discard error in the face of new light."

These passages are urging us to seek true knowledge through development of the individual mind, which will, according to the level attained, accept or reject information provided. Much of the present so-called knowledge of the universe is limited to mere theory, and does tend to make one's "reason revolt."

If one's "reason revolts" at these theories, to that particular individual, the teachings can only be accepted as erroneous, and one looks elsewhere for a solution. Through Silver Birch's teaching that "Matter only exists because of spirit," we can appreciate that this is the key to "make that which was incomprehensible easy to understand," and gives us the opportunity to observe the universe in a totally different light.

Bearing in mind the previous chapters on the human aura, it would perhaps be an interesting exercise to examine Darwin's theory of evolution, which has never been acceptable to me. You may liken my approach to theory, but at least it has a certain amount of scientific evidence to support it, and, in my estimation, is far more acceptable.

In 1858, Darwin postulated the theory that all animal and plant life on earth originate from a basic common source from which all life has evolved into its present form. This contradicts the teachings of Paul that "But God giveth it a body as it has pleased him, and to every seed a body. All flesh is not the same flesh, but there is one kind of flesh of men, another of flesh of beasts, another of fishes and another of birds."

Paul in relating individual "seeds" (auric field) to each species of "flesh bodies" (physical body), confirms my view of the manner in which reproduction of species is accomplished. Because of the "holographic" nature of the vital field of the male and female elements of any species, whether in the form of sperm and egg, pollen or other means of propagation, they merge and provide the pattern or mould of that particular species and the means of maintaining same.

Professor H.S Burr, in his research into "life fields," stated that "An acorn grows into an oak tree, a maize seed into a corn stalk and not a stalk of wheat or barley."

The only manner in which the form of matter can be altered is by changing the "seed" (auric field) pattern by such means as cross pollination or a mutual attraction between the fields concerned. The overall pattern cannot be changed genetically.

Like the animals in Noah's Ark, the origin and continuity of a species are dependant on a male and female to provide the chromosomes and genes for forming the physical body, and at the same time, the resultant combined vital field of the aura to mould and maintain the embryo .

To speak of evolution in terms of change in the original design of a physical form, in my view, is not possible. Apart from the occasional malformation within the chromosomes and genes of the male and female fertilising agent, the auric field remains identical with that of the species.

Cross pollination or fertilisation, will, if compatible, produce an auric field combining the qualities or otherwise of the participating parties. These, in turn, produce a mutation of both species. Natural selection within a species generally takes care of this problem. This raises the question of how Darwin's anthropoid evolved from an animal swinging through the trees to a human being capable of flying to the Moon in a matter of a mere 2,500,000 years.

Consider the fact that the horse remains within the same pattern of 600,000,000 years ago. The ant has not changed over 150,000,000 years whilst the fossilised remains of the dragonfly reveal that also has not changed over the last 300,000,000 years. Darwin's theory begins to look rather suspect. Wallace, an associate of Darwin, qualified the theory of evolution by stating, "Nature never over-endows species beyond the demands of everyday existence."

This approach — on the evidence of the development of the ant, the horse, the dragonfly and no doubt many other species — appeals to my common sense.

There is absolutely no necessity for the creatures of the earth, who are provided through their limited minds with all their requirements in terms of protection from the elements and provision of food, to improve their situation. Our so-called anthropoid ancestors had neither the incentive to improve their conditions nor the availability of a species approaching that of a human being to produce a mutation.

Genesis tends to be dismissed as mythical. In reality, it confirms my own vision of the manner in which the world was populated. In Genesis 1, 26-27, we have reference to the "religion" of Einstein "which reveals all intelligence of such superiority that, compared with it, all the systematic thinking and acting of human beings is an utterly insignificant reflection."

"And God said, let us make man in our image, after our

likeness; and let them have dominion over the fish of the sea and over the fowl of the air and over the cattle and over the earth and over every creeping thing that creepeth upon the earth. So God created man in his own image, in the image of God created he him; male and female created he them." In Matthew 19-4 Jesus emphasises this particular teaching "Have ye not read, that he which made them at the beginning made them male and female."

Because the term "we" is used, it is reasonable to assume that "God" is not of a singular nature, but a group of highly developed entities capable of carrying out the project of populating the world. Having provided male and female human beings, reproduction was guaranteed.

It would be natural to supervise the welfare of their creations by introducing at suitable intervals of time minds which can guide mankind towards a more civilised and peaceful way of life. If we accept the existence of various levels of intellectual awareness within the universe, it is not too difficult to visualise this scenario.

Reflecting on the introduction of human beings into this world of ours, perhaps the destruction of the prehistoric animals who once roamed the earth was more by design than accident. The human being, without any natural means of defence or physical baulk to deter predators, would have had much difficulty in surviving in a world where wild animals roamed at will.

Lacking the reproductive capacity of the majority of the creatures already installed upon the earth-plane — and the fact that the human offspring required more protection over a longer period of time than those of the creatures of the wild — the only solution was to provide human beings with a superior mind to that of the remainder of the inhabitants of the world.

Thus, the auric field of man was given an extra dimension, the celestial field, which provided him with guidance, and by attunement, knowledge. No doubt many attempts were made to establish mankind upon the earth which were terminated by disease, natural disasters or the inability to adapt to the conditions present at that particular time. This is reflected in the gaps existing in the palaeontological evidence available, the missing link, which never was.

The remains of some of the prototype models of man have been excavated from time to time. Science has assumed that a physical evolution brought about change in the skeletal remains. With the problems facing those attempting to place human beings in an inhospitable environment, one can appreciate the fact that it would take more than one attempt to create a model capable of living and maintaining itself under the then existing conditions.

Thus we have our earliest glimpse of man in his cave dwelling, with possibly paintings of deer, bison and birds decorating its walls. Like any experiment on similar lines, groups were distributed about the earth's surface in order to monitor and assess their performance under varying conditions.

From these widely distributed groups come legends of strange demi-gods who appeared within these groups who enlightened and taught various skills to primitive man. The description of these demi-gods varies in form, but their mission to man was identical — the progress of the human race. Physically, the description of some of these demi-gods sounds like fantasy, but faced with these characters today, might we not more fully comprehend the reason for their appearance?.

Hermes, or Mercury, arrived in the land we now know as Egypt and civilised the natives by giving them symbols to record sounds and ideas, numbers to count with, charts of the stars, herbs and remedies for ailments and means of producing music.

A fish-like monster known as Oannes presented himself to the primitive dwellers of Mesopotamia and taught them how to plant wheat, write down thoughts, count with numbers, build cities, compile laws and observe the stars.

His teaching skills were such that the people of the area became astronomers and mathematicians of note. In Mexico, "The Feathered Serpent," or Quetzalcoatl, descended from "A hole in the sky." He apparently travelled in a winged ship and instructed the inhabitants of Central America in agriculture, astronomy, architecture and a code of ethics.

From South America we hear of Viracocha, a tall white

man who imparted the high ethical ideals of civilisation to the Indian community. Orpheus arrived in ancient Greece and was said to possess such knowledge that he could answer any question. He spoke of strange incomprehensible things, such as the existence of life in the stars.

The fact that this knowledge was available and utilised by these various groups situated in wide, far flung areas of the world, is substantiated by the calendrical information available for the areas where civilisation began to flower.

The Codex Vaticanus A-3738 records the fact that the Maya's calendrical system commenced in 18,612 BC. In 11,542 BC, the Lunar calendar of Babylon and the Solar calendar of Egypt coincided. The calendrical computations of India commenced in 11,652 BC. However, compared with the writing of some of the more prominent sages of old, these calendrical dates are of quite recent vintage.

Hipparchus (190-125 BC) wrote of the Assyrian Chronicles stretching back 270,000 years. The Greek historian, Diogenes Laertius (third century AD) reveals that the astronomical records of the Egyptian priests commenced in 49,219 BC. Martianas Cappella (fifth century AD) confirms this by relating the fact that these same priests studied astronomy for over 40,000 years before enlightening humanity.

According to Simplicius (sixth century AD), these ancient Egyptians kept astronomical observations for 630,000 years. Cicero, although voicing his doubts, reported that the Archives of Babylon had their origin some 470,000 years prior to his treatise on the subject.

With these recorded dates and facts to hand, one can more fully comprehend the historical and scientific knowledge that was lost to civilisation in the destruction of the libraries of the cities of the Middle East and the South American centres of knowledge. One can but speculate on how much further advanced our knowledge would have been had it not suffered from the vandals of history.

The whole of civilisation as we know it today has been founded upon the work of the mathematicians, philosophers and men of science whose works escaped the destruction of these centres of learning.

Complemented by the inspiration received through outstanding scientists, artists, composers and law makers throughout history, we have fashioned a material civilisation but have not yet realised the source from which all inspiration derives, or the manner in which it may be tapped.

Silver Birch speaks of this relationship between the mind of man and the world of spirit in the following terms: "You must not regard the power of the spirit as it was expressed in any period of man's long history as being the final word in all divine revelation.

"Your world must realise that revelation is continuous and progressive, fitting itself to the stage of understanding of the people to whom it comes. It must not be so far ahead of them that they cannot understand it. It must only be so much in front that it is within their grasp.

"Always the wisdom of the power of the spirit is but one step ahead. When man achieves that step, he is ready for the next in the infinite ladder of wisdom...The amount of infinite knowledge you can receive is limited by the stage of development that you have spiritually and mentally reached.

"I make bold to claim that almost every boon in your world, every invention, and every discovery has its origin in the realms of spirit. The minds of your world are but the receptacles of the greater minds who use them to confer new benefits to your world of matter...

"You are executing plans which you have helped to create and to bring about in your own world. All the original work, if you like to use those words, is done in our world because all the energising, all the dynamic, originates, not with matter but with Spirit."

It is quite obvious to me that "evolution" is of the mind of the individual, not of a physical dimension. Man can create the material world, but the inspiration comes from the world of spirit. Darwin's theory of physical evolution is, in my opinion, one of "erroneous teachings" which have diverted our minds from the truth.

It is the teaching of Silver Birch in which he differentiates between the human being and the "beasts," in which category our friendly anthropoid is classed, which confirms my own view of the fallacy of Darwin's theory, "Wherever life takes conscious form, there you have individual spirit. That is the difference between you and the beasts. Man (the incarnate mind) is an individuated spirit, part of the Great Spirit."

Thus man's mind, functioning on a broad band width of vibrations, which gives him access to the world of spirit, has the advantage over animals. They merely possess sufficient intelligence to enable them to provide themselves with food and procreate. Their minds operate on a very narrow band width of vibrations.

How Darwin, who preached natural selection, could envisage the manner in which the physical evolution of man was accomplished, remains a mystery to me. Natural selection would suggest remaining within the species where the general sense of well-being and activity are reciprocated.

By merely examining the physiological differences between man and the anthropoid Darwin suggests we originate from, one gets the feeling that some of our scientists are more gullible than we think for there is little to substantiate the theory. Here is a brief survey of the physiological differences between man and anthropoid:

Man's brain, highly developed and constantly improving under the mind's influence, is far superior to that of the anthropoid.

There is no comparison between man's sensitive and flexible skin and the hairy hide of the anthropoid.

Man's highly flexible facial muscles can express his thoughts and feelings whereas the anthropoid has a very limited repertoire of expression.

Man's flexible, wide-ranging vocal chords, combined with the overted mucous lips and backed by a superior brain and mind, give him the greatest advantage over the limited faculties of the anthropoid in vocal terms

The dexterity displayed by the highly flexible and sensitive hands of man far outstrip the limitations of the anthropoid's hands.

Man's delicate, sensitive eyes tend to water at the ingress of foreign matter or merely at the emotions produced by mind and brain. This condition does not arise in the anthropoid.

With such a broad spectrum of physiological differences between man and his anthropoid "ancestors," and the lack of evidence available to substantiate Darwin's theory, I would suggest that if creatures such as the ant, dragonfly and horse remain replicas of the original pattern of hundreds of millions of years ago, the human being of today is basically a physical replica of our original forebears. There is no reason whatsoever why the species known as man should have defied the physical laws of nature in an accelerated leap in evolution when in reality the evolution was simply taking place within the mind of man himself.

To fellow travellers on the eternal journey to reality, I commend the words of Silver Birch: "You realise you are not creatures of chance, playthings of caprice, but part of the Infinite Spirit with an infinite power on which you can draw...

"Do not stop at any rung in the ladder of progress. It is only by imbibing, by striving to complete the picture, that life will be understood by you...

"Always the process of evolution has been at work. As the children of the Great Spirit have evolved and grown, so new teachers arose, new seers, new prophets and new visionaries, each with his visions, his dreams, his prophecies, his message, his inspiration, his truth, his teaching adapted to the needs of his day. There is no finality in revelation for the Great Spirit is perfect."

Chapter nine

"Natural law" and the universe

WE have speculated on the origin of man upon the earth-plane against the background of the teachings of Silver Birch, supported by scientific data of the part played by the fields of the aura.

Let us now apply the natural attributes of these fields to the universe as a whole. To enable us to get a perspective on the nature of the universe, we cannot better that provided by Silver Birch in the following passages, who, naturally, speaks with some authority:

"The Great Spirit is the natural Law of the universe. The Great Spirit is the creative force behind all life, whether registered in the plane of matter or that of the plane of spirit. The Great Spirit pervades all the universe, whether it is the tiny portion known to you or the larger part, which, as yet, has not been revealed to earthly gaze.

"Throughout the whole of your world and mine, throughout the universe, even in worlds that are not yet known to you, the laws of the Great Spirit reign supreme...Each one of you, all the human beings, not only on your planet but on millions of other planets, helps to constitute what I call God for the Great Spirit is the sum total of all spirit that is in the universe.

"The world is not ruled by chance; it is ruled by law and order. No matter where you turn, whether it be to attempt to comprehend the vastness of the interstellar spaces, whether you range with a telescope far over the horizons of the sky, or whether you take a microscope and begin to examine the small creations of life, all is subject to natural, unchangeable, immutable law. You are not a product of chance. Chance holds no place in an ordered universe where cause and effect follow one another with unalterable sequence.

"The power which fashioned all life provided rules or laws for its governance. It is perfect in its conception and organisation. These laws are spiritual laws because all life is spirit...The power of the spirit is invisible. It does not conform to any of the recognised standards of man. It has no length, it has no breadth, it has no height, it has no weight, it has no colour, it has no size, it has no taste, it has no smell...Nowhere through the labours of the scientist, or the chemist, or the physician, is to be discovered the motive power of life.

"The Great Spirit is almighty because all power is vested in the natural laws that control the universe and all the life in all the forms that exist in the universe...The power of the spirit is the power that breathed life into a world that was once all fire. The power of the spirit is the power which raised up man from the slime of the earth and endowed him with the qualities of divinity.

"The power of the spirit is the garment that the soul wears. The power of the spirit is the power which fashioned all life, which controls every motion and mutation of natural force, the power which regulates all the seasons and governs the growth of every seed, of every plant, of every flower, of every bush, of every tree, the power which is responsible for the whole scheme of evolution in all its intricate phases.

"I would point out the divine artistry of nature's handicraft. I would point to the stars, the diamonds in the sky. I would point to the glory of the sun, to the pale reflection of the moon. I would point to the whispering, murmuring breeze, to the nodding pines. I would point to the trickling stream and to the mighty ocean. I would touch every facet of nature showing how each is controlled by purpose, by law.

"I would add that where man has made any discovery in the field of natural life, he finds it comes within the orbit of law, that its growth is controlled and regulated, that it is part of one vast, intricate, yet harmonious pattern, that order reigns supreme throughout the vast universe, controlling planets and insects, storms and breezes, all life, no matter how variegated its expressions may be.

"When you consider, to take but one example, the myriads of creatures of varying sizes, shapes, colours and organisms, all of whom are provided with their sustenance by natural laws which overlook nothing, then you begin to see how truly comprehensive, how perfect in its conception and in its organisation is the law of the Great Spirit.

"There is no phase of motion, vibration, animal life, bird life, plant life, insect life, vegetable life, floral life, marine life, human life, spiritual life, that is not regulated by law. The universe is not discordant; it is one harmony on a grand scale. Once you perceive the key, the key that enables you to understand, it is very simple...The universal law controls all, and the law is the result of the Great Spirit."

What Silver Birch is making quite clear to us is that the Great Spirit, which is present in the universe as natural laws, controls the universe, and all that exists within it. Order and harmony reign supreme throughout the whole structure. There is not, within the whole of the universe, a thing of nature which does not respond to the intelligence provided by the immutable natural laws of the universe.

Thus from the smallest particle to the largest heavenly bodies in the universe, there is an intelligence present. It directs, manipulates and maintains that portion of matter, irrespective of size, which we observe at our particular level of existence.

As Silver Birch teaches: "The universe is not discordant. It is one harmony on a grand scale." If we consider the implications of this statement, it infers that the whole universe exists because there is harmony between all components of the system.

If all matter possesses an intelligence provided by natural law, the universe and everything we observe within it must be the result of natural attraction or repulsion. If we liken this to an experiment with magnet and iron filings, we can observe that the filings take up a mutual pattern with the individual field of the magnet.

This brings us back to the electromagnetic fields which surround all matter and defined by Professor Herbert L.Konig in the following terms, "Sufficient evidence, direct and indirect, exists, pointing to the fact that electromagnetic forces in general provide the means of transferring information between or to living organisms."

If we compliment this statement with that of Dr Walter Kroy that "These fields provide electromagnetic signals which are short enough to penetrate the skin structure," etc, we can realise that the whole structure of the universe is dependent on the information provided by means of photons in the electromagnetic vital field of each individual species or object.

The information, in a computer-like manner within each individual field, provides, through natural law or the Great Spirit, the object or species with sufficient knowledge to enable it to take physical form. If necessary, the knowledge enables a particular species to be aware of any special requirements in the food chain and method of procreation.

That is the limitation placed on the lower forms of life. Because we are, through the field of our mind, spiritually part of the Great Spirit or Supreme Intelligence of the universe, we have free will. This gives us a greater choice of the manner in which we live, eat and manipulate our lives.

Procreation of all species is accomplished through the "holographic" nature (the part is a replica of the whole) of the auric field or fields of the participating species.

Thus with chromosomes and genes provided within the species, and the food supply available to nourish, the vital field possesses all the ingredients necessary to mould and maintain the form of that particular species. Through these vital fields of matter, the natural laws maintain order throughout the universe.

The physicist, investigating the microcosmic world with all his elaborate equipment, is correct to a degree in declaring that all appears to be random chance, but it is the fields of the unruly quarks, leptons, gluons, hadrons, etc, which decide the particular form of matter they will assume.

I would suggest the following teachings of Silver Birch would compliment the foregoing passages: "God is in you as God is in the rain, the sun, the flowers, vegetables, in animals, in all that has any aspect of existence, however small it may be...The Great Spirit is within everything. Everything is the Great Spirit. Because the soul knows itself, the Great Spirit knows the soul. Because the sparrow is the Great Spirit, the Great Spirit knows the sparrow. Because the Great Spirit is in the trembling leaf, the trembling leaf is the Great Spirit."

The source of micro energies is the Sun which, through solar activity, creates magnetic field strengths of up to 4,000 gauss and provides a continuous stream of protons (hydrogen nuclei) and electrons together with a few helium nuclei, which are constantly emitted in all directions.

These products are borne away on the solar wind which has long been suspected for a number of reasons, among them the link between solar activity and changes in the Earth's magnetic field. The astronomer will freely admit that solar magnetism is, in fact, the controlling factor in a wide variety of solar phenomena. Like the physicist, he is quite correct, but until they get to grips with the reality of the nature of these electromagnetic fields, they will never understand what makes our solar system tick.

Condensing the conclusions of Professor Herbert L.Konig on the nature of electromagnetic field of the Earth, we have the following description. The field consists of the electrically charged components of matter, generated by radiation from the Sun.

This functions over the entire frequency range from the ultraviolet and X-ray in particular to infra-red and microwave which are deflected around the Earth by the terrestrial magnetic field. Thus, in the magnetic field of the Earth we have a similar electromagnetic range to that observed in the auric field of the human being, which immediately introduces a common factor.

This being the case, it is not difficult to accept that the Earth's magnetic field, which traps the electromagnetic/ energy particles of the solar wind into the Magnetosphere, acts as the auric field of planet Earth. This keeps it gently turning and providing the necessary intelligence for the reproduction of all forms of life upon the planet.

When we look to the heavens, our solar system continues to progress harmoniously as it has done for millions of years, with the planets turning on their axis at the exact speed they have always maintained while continuing in the same precise orbit. When these planets can be timed to a fraction of a second in the course of their revolutions over a period of a year, there is no question of random chance existing within the structure of the universe controlled by natural law.

Dr Walter Kroy indicates that "Electromagnetic signals are the primary language of atoms and molecules and, with a somewhat shifted spectrum of larger units." These "larger units," I would suggest, include the planets of our solar system and the universe at large.

Recapping the work of Professor Konig to illustrate the relationship of the Earth's magnetic field to the auric field of the human being, we are acquainted with the fact that "Low frequency signals are extensive in terms of their wavelength and penetrate entire organic substances, more in terms of magnetic fields...

"The signal stimulus is present all over the body (Earth), in micro-wave radiation or radiation within the extended light frequency range, can aim at and reach a particular part of the body (Earth), a particular receptor, but only when the receptor is on or near the surface of the body (Earth).

"It is also conceivable that bio-information could be transmitted on from there, with a corresponding time lag, to deeper laying regions of the body (Earth), irrespective of the direction of the incoming radiation."

Through the process of dowsing, we are introduced, in my opinion, to the "receptors" and means of transmitting the incoming information to the deeper laying regions of planet Earth.

In "The Secret Country," Janet and Colin Bord ask the question, "What is the nature of the energy involved and for what purpose is it used?...Radionics is concerned with the balanced flow of subtle energies through the various levels of being that make man, thereby ensuring perfect health and vitality. This principle must also apply to all other living forms, including our planet, which is no less alive than we are."

This suggests that because the human body requires nourishment and knowledge to sustain it, it must be a law of nature or principle that other living forms and our planet have similar requirements to sustain life. Because we have a scientific concept of the nature of the auric or electromagnetic fields of matter, we can appreciate the manner in which this is accomplished.

Guy Underwood, in "The Pattern of the Past," suggests that a principle of nature exists which is unknown to, or unidentified by, science.

Its main characteristics are that it appears to be generated within the Earth, and causes wave motion perpendicular to the Earth's surface; that it has great penetrative power; that it affects the nerve cells of animals; that it forms spiral patterns; and is controlled by mathematical laws involving principally the numbers three and seven. Until it is otherwise identified, I shall refer to it as the Earth force. It could be an unknown principle, but it seems more likely that it is an unrecognised effect of some already established force, such as magnetism or gravity.

The "Earth force" manifests itself in lines of discontinuity, which I call geodetic lines, which form a network on the surface of the Earth. The lower animals instinctively perceive and use these lines. Their behaviour is considerably affected by them.

Man is similarly affected, but less strongly, and cannot usually perceive the lines without artificial assistance. Underwood's Geodetic System, plotted by dowsing, comprises a complex system of water lines and secondary patterns upon which is sited ancient structures which mark significant geodetic features of the system.

In a similar manner to man's physical body, we now have "receptors" provided by the ancient structures. These supply the nerve network of planet Earth with nourishment and intelligence, in all its various forms, via its magnetic or electromagnetic field. The nature of this "Earth force" can be appreciated from the experiences of the following investigators into the phenomenon of dowsing megalithic structures.

Andrew Davidson, researching stone circles, "found that each stone is predominantly positive or negative and oppositely charged to its neighbour. There are polarity changes six days after the new moon."

On one such occasion he experienced the change whilst

dowsing at a circle. His pendulum slowly stopped, and then gained momentum in the opposite direction, "the whole sequence taking seven minutes. Stones can also have a combined influence, and their layout is probably of great importance."

T.C.Lethbridge in "The Legend of the Sons of God," speaks of his experience at the stone circles known as the Merry Maidens, near Lamorna, Cornwall:

"As the pendulum started to swing, a strange thing happened. The hand resting on the stone received a strong tingling sensation like a mild electric shock and the pendulum itself shot out until it was circling nearly horizontal to the ground.

"The stone itself, which must have weighed over a ton, felt as if it was rocking and almost dancing about. This was quite alarming, but I stuck to my counting...The next day I sent my wife up alone to see what happened to her. She had the same experience."

John Williams, an experienced dowser, has had several experiences in which he has been thrown back from the stones when placing his hands upon them. He described the force involved as spiral-like, building up through the whole body and throwing the person touching it back from the stone. In the case of Lethbridge, this force was reflected in the pendulum circling almost horizontal to the ground, but instead of his physical body being thrown back from the stone, the stone commenced "rocking and almost dancing."

Vera Stanley Alder in "The Initiation of The World" describes the etheric body (auric field) of man in the following terms: "Where great activity and condensed structures in the etheric body (electromagnetic field) is located we get a plexus...

"A close latticework of nerves forming a nucleus...and at the heart of the nucleus we find in the etheric body (electromagnetic field) a vital vortex or 'centre,' which is expressed in the flesh as an endocrine gland" (chakra).

There is not much difficulty in recognising the fact that the same method of conveying information to man's physical is employed in the maintenance of planet Earth.

We can now begin to understand, through the nature of the electromagnetic fields of life, which provide the means of storing and retrieving information, the words of Silver Birch, "The power of the spirit is the power which fashioned all life, which controls every motion and mutation of natural force."

An appreciation of the manner in which the "Earth force" provides the means of "controlling every motion" may be obtained by recapping the nature of the human aura and relating it to the geodetic lines forming a network on the surface of Earth. Because the features of the human body and planet Earth have been of a similar nature, there is no reason to consider that any difference exists in the properties of the respective electromagnetic fields.

Dr E.K.Muller defines these properties as follows: 1. The force field is not electrical in nature as we understand the term, but can be measured in terms of electromagnetic dynamics. 2. The force fields can change non-conductors to conductors. 3. The force fields can pass through glass, mica, copper and tinfoil.

Thus, although the dowser speaks in terms of positive and negative, this is only in respect of the response of the pendulum to the energy prevailing in the "Earth force" and that of the field of the operator. Dowsing research has, however, shown that positive and negative energies alternate in the geodetic lines on the Earth's surface, and because of their properties of changing non-conductors to conductors form a continuous network.

The controlling factor within these lines of energy prevent these lines from interacting with each other. The fact that Andrew Davidson observed a change of polarity in the "Earth force" six days after a new moon indicates the presence of an intelligent manipulation of the geodetic lines.

From dowsing sources, there appears to have been a detailed survey made of these geodetic lines of the "Earth force," which reveals they are formed by two separate systems. These have been designated "The Curry and Hartmann Grid Nets."

The Curry grid lines are approximately 3.5 metres to 4 metres apart in mid-Europe and 4-5 metres at the Equator. This grid net is orientated at 45 degrees to the Hartmann net pattern, i.e. NW to SE and SW to NE, spanning the whole globe. The lines are polarised in terms of positive and negative dowsing reaction, with defined width and radiation waves and considered to be of terrestrial origin (magna radiation, earth magnetism, etc).

The Hartmann grid lines are approximately 2 metres and 2.5 metres apart, the grid pattern being orientated NS and EW, which spans the whole globe. This grid, considered to be of cosmic origin, is subject to a phase change of energies every six hours, at which time slight variations when changing polarities may be observed.

Where positive and negative lines cross in either network, the electromagnetic nature of the force merely produces a neutral junction. The idea of a force functioning through an electromagnetic field in such a manner recalls the words of Silver Birch, "Nowhere through the labours of the scientist, or the chemist, or the physician, is to be discovered the motive power of life."

Although our knowledge of the actual "life force" is limited, we can speculate, through the information we have gleaned of the nature of the electromagnetic fields surrounding all matter, the manner in which the fields of the respective grids react upon each other.

The Curry grid may be considered a fixed electromagnetic system on the surface of the globe which is overlaid by the Hartmann grid, and subject to variations in phase changes in energies.

This, to our limited knowledge of the energies we are dealing with, would seem to provide a propulsion system for planet Earth, through the forces functioning within the combined grid nets, providing the torque required to keep it rotating in space like a huge gyroscope. Through the fluctuating phase changes of energy within the Hartmann grid, we can sense the control of the Great Spirit through the programmed electromagnetic field of planet Earth, equating with that of the vital field of man.

Without unduly stretching one's imagination, by accepting the existence of electromagnetic fields about all physical matter, there is the common factor of vortices of power — centred on receptors — which provide in the case of Earth's creatures, the information required for the development and maintenance of the physical body and, from a cosmic view, the information required to control and maintain the motion of all the bodies of the universe and the welfare of all forms of life which dwell thereon. Thus, throughout the universe, the whole structure, from the most minute to the mightiest, is subject to the information provided by the Universal Intelligence, or Great Spirit, in a computer-like manner, within the electromagnetic fields surrounding all matter.

Thus, throughout the whole structure of the universe, we have the equivalent of the vital body which moulds and maintains a particular form of matter, and a body elemental which provides the means of sustaining and reproducing matter in terms of food and procreation.

This covers the animal, vegetable and mineral kingdoms as a whole, but man, as we are now aware, also possesses, at a higher vibration, the field of the mind, the incarnate spirit. The incarnate spirit of man, as Silver Birch so aptly expresses it, is part of the Universal Intelligence or Great Spirit:

"As life becomes individuated in human beings, God is expressed in individuality as well as the natural forces that are part of the universe, which, in turn, is part of the cosmos...

"I want to make it quite clear that you, as human beings, are within the framework of the Great Spirit, and have an access to it because you contribute a vital part to it...That is the difference between you and the lower beasts. Man is an individuated spirit, part of the Great Spirit."

Now we can fully comprehend the remark attributed to Jesus that "Ye are Gods" for each individual incarnate spirit possesses the attributes of "God" to a degree commensurate with the spiritual development of the mind, which can influence the universe at an appropriate level. It is the level at which the majority of humanity functions that is reflected in the general conditions prevailing upon the planet.

Therefore, it is only through educating Earth's inhabitants in the benefits of harmonious co-existence that our standard of life can be improved. Thus man, because he represents the intelligence of the Great Spirit at this level of perception, has the collective husbandship of the planet and the personal responsibility to the universe and all life within it.

Having come to appreciate the difference between the controlling factors of man and beast, it would be of interest to study the manner in which the mind of the lower forms of life, which correspond to our body elementals, respond to the environment in which they find themselves. Because of the rather short life span of many species, progeny has to develop with little or no assistance from parents. It follows that the mind of each individual species must be programmed to carry out a routine of feeding, procreating and dying in very limited periods of time.

Let us consider that among the signal stimulus received by the Earth's receptors there are those which provide each form of life upon it with sufficient knowledge — no more, no less — to enable these forms to live and reproduce. We have previously considered the manner in which signal stimulus can form, control and maintain physical bodies involving the use of billions of minute signals.

Now let us apply this principle to planet Earth and the stimulating signals provided by the earth forces of the dowser. Guy Underwood, from his research into the properties of these forces, concluded that they "affect the nerve cells of animals."

Let us consider these earth forces functioning through the geodetic system of the Earth acting as one communication path for simultaneously carrying a number of channels for transmission of information.

This could, by carrier frequency, in which each channel corresponds to a different carrier frequency — or to be more precise, a different frequency range of vibrations, similar in nature to those within the auric field — supply each individual form of life with the basic information necessary for its procreation, form and maintenance. This analogy requires a modulator, which we can assume to be incorporated in the terrestrial magnetic field and the demodulator incorporated into the electromagnetic or auric field of each individual life form.

This source provides a behavioural pattern, or what we would term, "natural instinct," to all forms of life. If it were not for the presence of the mind's field within the human aura, we would be responding, via the physical brain, to the influence of the body elemental, placing us on the level of the animals.

White Eagle identifies the body elemental as follows: "This is not an evil thing; it has its place in evolution, not only of man, but also the lower forms of life...Man has to learn in the course of his evolution that the higher self must gain complete domination over the body elemental."

Silver Birch states that "whether you take a microscope and begin to examine the small creations of life, all is subject to natural, unchangeable, immutable law. You are not a product of chance." Here, he is categorically stating that all matter obeys the instructions provided for its welfare, irrespective of form. I therefore consider the term "natural instinct" an insult to the intelligence provided by the Great Spirit, the Universal Intelligence.

In the simpler forms of life which can be observed without recourse to a microscope, we have the larva, a free-living animal, quite different in appearance from the adult. The most familiar examples are caterpillars, the larvae of moths and butterflies. These free-living animals are the result of fertilisation of an egg of the species in the course of mating. It then deposited by the female upon a particular type of vegetation which will sustain the larva until the final change to adult, when it can display its beauty.

Through the whole process from egg, larva to adult, and the individual style of courtship and mating related to the species for procreation, there is no indication of external guidance being introduced. This alone would suggest that the manner in which the complete cycle is effected in such a short period of time is due more to the functioning of a programmed mind rather than a loosely termed "natural instinct."

Programming is reflected throughout nature in the billions of differing life forms upon our earthplane and the processes employed by which fertilisation takes place for the renewal of species.

When one perceives the manner in which the whole of nature is dependent on each other for its continued existence, one can comprehend that if all were not "subject to natural, unchangeable, immutable laws" or programmed minds, the universe as we know it would not exist.

Plant life reveals some of the more complicated methods of fertilisation in which insects and birds play their part in pollination. This process often involves one species of insect or bird being responsible for the pollination of an individual plant. Animals are pretty stereotyped in their approach to procreation within their own species as indeed are birds. The individuality of the programmed mind is reflected more in the social behaviour adopted by each species, especially birds.

The various species of birds have their own courtship behaviour, generally emphasised by ritual display which can be bizarre and complicated, or brief and sketchy. There is also a vast difference in the style and method of construction of the nests of the individual species. These vary from a few sticks on the ground to the intricate nests of the Weaver Bird or African Hammer-Headed Stork.

What are in some cases very intricate and delicate operations are loosely termed "natural instincts." But as the progeny of all bird-life commence as an egg, and within a few weeks have to fend for themselves, one would expect the instinct to be of a more general character.

The cuckoo lays its egg in the nest of a different species of bird, who hatches and rears the chick, but due to the programmed mind of the cuckoo, it continues to perpetuate its species in a replica of the parents.

The inhabitants of the sea have various methods of reproduction, feeding and behaving according to species. Flat fish such as the Dab and Plaice are hatched-shaped like the majority of other fish, with an eye each side of its head, but a month later, begin to metamorphosis into a flat fish. Within two and a half weeks, its left eye has moved over to the right side of the head. Could one term this action "natural instinct" or, as in the case of the larva, a "programmed mind"?

The herd instinct within many species is due to the narrow band-width of vibration upon which their minds function. Because the species, to all intents and purposes, share a common restricted and limited mind, the response time between members of the herd is much less than that of the individual minds of the human race.

This produces a high level of telepathy within the herd, causing a swift response to danger and the intricate movement of shoals of fish and flights of birds. A thought generated in the mind of one member of the herd is almost immediately picked up and acted upon by the remainder.

Along with the information provided for the day-to-day behavioural pattern of each individual species comes that which gives direction to the migration of those creatures who have need of it. Whether animal, fish or bird, their movements are controlled and guided by a source of intelligence within the earth force of the geodetic system.

Thus, in the same manner as a dowser mentally attunes his mind field with that of the ley lines, minerals, etc, to produce a physical reaction in the divining instrument, the mind field of a particular life form interacts with the appropriate frequency within the earth force relative to that particular species, producing an automatic physical response.

Much speculation is made of the ability of migrating creatures utilising the sun and stars as aids to navigation. The fields of the celestial bodies could possibly influence the mind fields of these creatures to a degree, but the main source of information is provided by the earth force.

Returning to our friend the cuckoo, we can appreciate through the migration cycle of this particular species that a programmed mind is very much in evidence. The parent cuckoos reach Europe from Africa in the spring.

The female lays her eggs in the nests of other birds, leaving the foster parents to rear the baby cuckoo who, without further ado, dispatches the progeny of the host parents. The young cuckoo never see their own parents, who migrate back to Africa in July. A month later, the young cuckoos — of their own accord — take the same migration path without any external assistance from parents or adults.

Thus the source of the behavioural pattern of all species stems from the associated fields of the earth force which, although related to reproduction and sex drive, is not evil. In species other than human, this can be qualified as generally speaking each species has a rigid code of conduct to which it adheres and brings it into coincidence with the whole of nature.

In possessing a field of the mind which represents the accumulated experiences of the incarnating entity, because it has free will, humanity is the only species upon this planet which can bring about and maintain a state of disharmony, which is in direct opposition to the harmony of the Great Spirit.

My views on those who choose the path of disharmony are not as charitable as that of Silver Birch. I therefore give way to the more illuminating words of that great teacher:

"You either live your life as an individual, as a class, as a nation, as a world, in harmony with the law, or contrary to the law. If you live contrary to the law, you get all the results: darkness, disease, difficulty, chaos, bankruptcy, misery and bloodshed. But if you live in harmony with the law, you enjoy all the fruits of the spirit, all its wisdom, knowledge, understanding, truth, justice, equity and peace.

"You are not an automaton. You have free will, true, within restricted limits, but you have to make your decision. This is true of individuals and nations. Those who choose to live with the law, those who adopt the law of service to one another as their rule, automatically reap the results from nature and the universe.

"We are concerned with deeds, with actions and with the life that every individual lives. We teach the supreme law of cause and effect; that none thwarts the Great Spirit, that none cheats the law, that man is his own saviour and his own redeemer. That man pays the penalty for every wrong doing and that man reaps the reward for every kindness that he performs.

"We say that the laws of the Great Spirit are mechanical, automatic in their action; that kindness, tolerance, sympathy and service automatically make you the better because you have practised them, and that selfishness, wrong-doing and intolerance automatically make you worse.

"You cannot alter that inflexible law. There is no cheap reprieve. There are no easy pardons. Divine justice rules the whole universe. A spiritual dwarf cannot be a spiritual giant. There is no death-bed repentance.

"Millions of people think the world in which they live is the only world. They think the life they are living is the only life they will live so they try to accumulate all the things of matter, the earthly treasures which one day they will have to leave behind.

"The cause of your wars, bloodshed, misery, sickness —

practically all of them — is due to the fact that the secret of life eludes millions who do not know that they are eternal spiritual beings here and now, that they are not bodies only. They are spirits expressing themselves through bodies. They are placed in a world of matter to grow and to develop that soul which will fit them for their real home which begins from the moment the Angel of Death touches them on the shoulder and says, 'Come hither.'

"You can provide all the conditions. If the soul does not desire to grow, you can do nothing. All you can do is to spread knowledge, driving out ignorance, driving out bigotry, driving out prejudice. Spread knowledge. Sometimes it will fall on stony ground, but very often it reaches receptive soil and the tiny seed that you have dropped will blossom.

"Our task is to spread the light wherever we can. Gradually the rays of truth will illuminate your world and all that belongs to the darkness of superstition, all that makes for ugliness and squalor, will be transformed as man desires to see conditions about him fit for the particles of the Great Spirit to dwell in.

"You must try to understand that a good deal of the ugliness and evil exists because of the vested interests of those who find it pays them to build slums, those who are interested only in the money they can make, who are unconcerned with what happens to their brothers as long as they line their own pockets. The evil often results from the sordid conditions into which these people are plunged.

"But then you must remember that man is infinite, that the whole of life is a struggle from darkness towards the light, from the lower towards the higher, from the lesser towards the greater, that through evolution man's spirit is constantly rising. If there were no struggle, if there were no distress, then there would be nothing for the spirit to conquer.

"The paramount need of today is for the dissemination of these simple truths, assurance of the life beyond the grave, assurance that you are never friendless, neglected or lonely, assurance that there is an overruling, guiding, beneficent power filled with the warmth of divine love.

"These are the simple truths of the spirit that will stand forever. They will answer every test that reason demands.

They will not demean your intelligence. They are simple, so simple, that they can be grasped and understood by any ordinary individual...We say that service, the exercise of the spirit, deeds which are unselfish and altruistic, the attempt to help those less fortunate than yourself, giving strength to the weak, removing the load off the shoulders of those who have much to carry —all this to us is religion.

"At present there is no recognition of this eternal fact that primarily you are spiritual beings, none of whom can live in isolation from others, that your evolution is bound up with one another, that you advance or retreat collectively.

"This is your responsibility. I have always said that knowledge brings responsibility as to how it is to be employed. Once you are aware of spiritual truths, once you are familiar with the workings of the power of the spirit, you should have no fear of today or the morrow.

"The Law is that you are put here to develop your spirit so that it can grow and grow. It never stops growing in your world or mine...Earth is your schoolhouse of experience. It is not perfect, neither are you. You are imperfect beings in an imperfect world trying to express as much of perfection as you can while you are there...

"There is no ugliness in our world, except in those very low spheres, of course, where dwell the people whose lives were so impoverished that they have no beauty to enhance their conditions here. But with that exception of the grey spheres, evil and ugliness have no existence in a world where the causes of evil and ugliness have been removed."

One can imagine living in a world where the wheat has been sifted from the chaff, where there is not constant aggravation generated by others who, in the many outlets of expression available to them, create vibrations of disharmony.

Only through educating the masses in the true nature of the universe can we hope to bring about change upon the earth-plane through the improvement in the level of morality, in all its aspects, within the mind of man.

Without that knowledge, we shall continue to drift collectively towards the "grey spheres" through the regression of the spirit rather than its progression. In the situation we find ourselves at this level of development, we have our free will to determine our future progress, or otherwise. Let us make certain we use our free will to ensure a future of unparalleled harmony and beauty through service to others.

Chapter ten

Science and the electromagnetic aura

THE greatest tragedy of the last century has been the inability of scientists investigating the auric or electromagnetic field of mankind to capitalise on the research work of their predecessors. There has been, in my estimation, sufficient knowledge available regarding the nature of the field to have progressed much further than science has today.

It has not been my intention to present a totally scientific approach to the teachings of Silver Birch as there are many other aspects of the fields which makes one aware of the manner in which the electromagnetic fields of life can be influenced, for good or bad, by external electromagnetic fields or chemical pollution.

I do not propose going into this subject in great depth, but will give a résumé of the conclusions reached by some of the more prominent researchers in this field in order that readers may assume a more informed opinion of the nature of the universe in which they dwell.

Informing your personal view of the nature of the universe, remember the words of Silver Birch: "Do not hedge yourself around and refuse to allow new inspiration to come to you. Truth is a constant search...There is no new truth. Truth is truth. There is knowledge which depends on the individual being ready to receive it."

Dr Walter J. Kilner. Known more for his dicyanin screen, he conducted many experiments into the nature of the auric field in which he concluded that:

1. Three separate radiations surrounding the physical body are discerned by use of the Kilner screen.

2. By studying the condition of the aura, diagnosis of the state of the physical body may be obtained.

3. The size and colour of the aura is influenced by health conditions.

4. The aura may be expanded and the colours influenced by will power.

5. The aura responds to a negative or positive electrical charge.

6. Magnetic fields can influence the depth of the aura, and in some experiments, produce distress in the subject.

7. The brilliance of the aura fades under hypnosis.

8. Vapours of various chemicals adversely affect the aura.

9. As death approaches, the aura gradually decreases and finally disappears.

Dr V.M Inyushin. A biophysicist at Kazakh State University, Alma-Ato, former USSR, concluded that:

1. Bioplasma (auric field) is the matrix of the biological field, which he describes as a "frozen in hologram," each fragment possessing the characteristics of the essential properties of the whole.

2. The bioplasma cannot cease to breathe in rhythm with the cosmos.

Professor Wlodzimierz Sedlak. Researching bioplasma bodies at the Catholic University of Lublin, he concluded:

1. Bioplasma (auric fields) is the basis of all chemical and electron processes.

2. Bioplasma is the carrier of all information within systems.

3. Life can be ultimately be reduced to the conception of plasma/electromagnetic fields.

Dr E.K. Muller. In his experiments with a Fortin

magnetometres atmospherique et medical, he determined that:

1. A force field (auric field) exists external to the physical body, which may be varied in strength through the rate of circulation of the blood, in conjunction with the quality of same, determined by the calorific value of the food consumed, physical exercise or mere will power.

2. The force field is not electrical in nature as we understand the term, but can be measured in terms of electromagnetic dynamics.

3 The force field can change non-conductors to conductors.

4. The force field can pass through glass, mica, copper and tinfoil.

Professor H.S.Burr. An American biologist, studied the "life," or auric fields of nature, over a period of 30 years, and came to the following conclusions:

1. Man and all forms are ordered and controlled by electrodynamic "life," or auric fields, which provide the means of moulding and maintaining the universe and all within it.

2. The life is primary and provides the "myriads of consequences" seen in nature. In other words, provides the control factor (DNA) which distinguishes the many facets existing within the universe.

3. Mind does not exist in time or space and requires no energy transformations, but exists within a regulated field which is unique to each individual.

4. Life, or auric fields, are links in a "chain of authority," from the simplest form to the most complex.

5. One "life" or auric field cannot exist within another similar field without interaction taking place and producing results of great significance.

6. "Life" or auric fields which control all forms are irrefutable evidence of the existence of law and order within the Universe.

7. The functioning of the nervous system is derived from dynamic forces imposed on cell groups by the total field pattern.

8. Conditions existing within the physical body may be monitored through these fields.

The following members of the scientific fraternity sub-scribe to the work of the International Institute of Biophysics, Kaiserslautern, Germany, of which Dr Fritz Albert Popp is one of the managing directors:

Dr Helmut Breithaup. 1. Holography is a process by which the entire information generated by the physical body can be stored and retrieved as required, external to that body.

Professor Herbert L.Konig. 1. The electrically charged components of matter, generated by radiation from the Sun, function over the entire frequency range from ultraviolet and X-ray in particular to infra-red and microwave.

2. Sufficient evidence, direct and indirect, exists pointing to the fact that electromagnetic forces, in general, provide the means of transferring information between, or to, living organisms.

3. The signal stimulus is present all over the body, but it is in the microwave radiation or radiation in the extended light frequency which can target a particular receptor on or near the body surface and relay the bio-information to the inner regions of the body, irrespective of the direction of the incoming radiation signal.

Dr Walter Kroy. 1. Stimulation of certain regions of the body surface of human beings and animals produces reactions within the internal organs.

2. Electromagnetic fields in the ultraviolet, visible and infra-red ranges surround the bodies of both humans and animals. These fields provide electromagnetic signals which are short enough to penetrate the skin structure with moderate absorption in selected areas of the body surface.

These signals appear to be responsible for fundamental regulatory functions by passing information through the contact regions to the organ cells via the connecting tissue. The organs in turn, using a similar system, communicate internally.

3. Electromagnetic signals are the primary language of atoms and molecules and, with a somewhat shifted spectrum, of larger units.

Dr Fritz Albert Popp. 1. One may assume that the replication and transcription of a DNA section is governed by interaction with the electromagnetic field, and that the strength and quality of the signal assigned to different tissues and cells will vary.

2. The biological system exhibits "holographic" properties in the manner in which receptors of various organs may be located in other organs, such as the ear, the hands, the eyes, acupuncture and iris diagnosis.

3. The assumption that the information of the DNA is stationarily delocalised over the body also reflects the "holographic" properties within the biological system.

Dr Ulrich Warnke and Dr Fritz Albert Popp. 1. Electric and magnetic fields are mutually transformable and principally not different.

2. Weak magnetic fields influence biological systems in terms of cell growth and movement, ageing, life span and activity of organisms.

3. The central nervous system can also be influenced by magnetic fields with frequencies of extremely narrow band widths and low amplitude.

4. The healing of damaged or diseased tissue can be accelerated by the application of suitable magnetic field intensity and frequency range.

5. Alternating magnetic fields of certain amplitudes at variable frequencies in the ELF and VLF range are accepted in medical practice today.

Semyon Kirlian (Meritorious Inventor, Former USSR). Although not of academic material, Kirlian, a member of the technical staff at Krasnoder Hospital, using a rebuilt Tesla high frequency generator producing 200 KV, proceeded to capture on film "the very spark of life that animates all living bodies from plant to man, in all its luminous vibrant colours." From research in conjunction with his wife, Valentina, one may deduce the following:

1. The auric field can be photographed in colour by Kirlian photography.

2. Thoughts and emotions produced within the mind are reflected in the changing state and colour of the auric field monitored through Kirlian photography.

3. Health conditions may be monitored through Kirlian photography.

4. The action of high voltage/ high frequency charges on the auric field can bring about deterioration of the physical body.

5. The contour of the aura of a leaf, and therefore possibly any living body, remains intact upon removing a section of same.

Viewing some of our TV documentaries, I often feel how much more progress medical science could make if it really understood the laws governing the fields of the aura.

To illustrate this point, I would like to refer to the documentary "Doctor from Kurgan." The main character, a Soviet orthopaedic surgeon, devised a series of cage-like structures which were designed to fit over various parts of limbs. With these contrivances, malformed limbs could be reshaped and lengthened as necessary. The method employed in this work is to ensure that the bone of the limb to be reshaped or repaired is in two parts.

A cage which is fitted with two adjustable flanges is placed over the limb and pins inserted through the flanges into each section of bone in order to regulate the distance between the ends of the two sections.

"Miraculously," the bone structure and blood vessels grow across the gap to complete the repair. This process enables deformed limbs to be reshaped in order to give mobility to the patient.

Exercise is deemed to be essential to the whole process, and the rigidity of the metal cages allows the patients to commence active exercises within two days of their operations with a view to accelerating the healing process.

There we are witnessing the controlling photon emissions of a particular limb within the vital field of the aura, continuing its function of maintaining the pattern of the physical body (Professor H.S.Burr). The exercises undertaken strengthen the field of the aura (Dr E.K Muller) and reduces the recovery time.

Here in Britain, external sources providing electromagnetic stimulation of the auric field have been utilised to accelerate healing, but possibly at the expense of longer periods of hospitalisation.

One other documentary that comes readily to mind is that of an alternative method of quickly diagnosing the allergies of patients with various medical conditions. This method required the patient to hold phials, one at a time, each containing a different substance, to their cheek, noting any reaction.

However, when requested to explain the manner in which he obtained such accurate diagnosis without any of the substances actually touching the physical body, he was at a loss.

The answer obviously lies in Dr E.K.Muller's experiments which concluded that "The force field (auric field) can pass through glass, mica, copper and tinfoil." Therefore, the patient's aura's vital field penetrates the glass phial and samples its contents. The reactions are noted on his or her physical body.

From the minor illustrations provided, one can realise that once the nature of the auric fields are comprehended, a totally new universe will be revealed. The physicist has already as much knowledge of his particles and atoms, necessary for our welfare whilst the atom-smasher at CERN has only been an expensive luxury. Knowing that atomic material is programmed to function in conjunction with "life," or auric fields of creation, should give the physicist a new lease of life.

The medical profession would also benefit as the bio-engineers devised new models of treatment through controlling the fields of the aura rather than the use of drugs.

With the know-how and equipment we have today, I have not much doubt that communication based on TV screens, etc, could be established within the higher ranges of vibration with those who have effected their transition.

Above all, perhaps through scientific proof of the progressive nature of the human spirit in terms of other states of consciousness, thoughts that this world is the be-all and end-all of all life will be dispelled. This, one would hope, will lead to a complete revisal of the moral and spiritual values of humanity throughout the world.

Knowledge of the properties of the aura's field has been available to the scientific world for many years, but progress in the field of electromagnetic biology seems to be remarkably slow considering the modern instruments, equipment and knowledge at their disposal today.

I would agree it is necessary to subject some of the experiments and conclusions reached by previous researchers to modern techniques, but only with a view to confirming their conclusions. Although the equipment utilised may not be of the same standard of today, the principles have been established, and should stand today. Perhaps this lack of progress can be related to Silver Birch's summing up of the situation:

"What does happen is that sometimes there is a development of the brain, but not a development of the mind or the spirit, and then you have people who are intellectual but it does not follow that because they are intellectual they are great souls or that they have great minds.

"It is a progress that is limited strictly to the physical thing, the brain, and sometimes it is true that amongst those people there are those who reject anything but the complicated. But where there is true progress, the progress of the mind and the soul, then the progress brings a greater awareness of spiritual realities for it is a mental and spiritual development. In those cases you get a discarding of the former erroneous conceptions and a closer approximation to the truth."

As a layman, I have presented the scientific facts I am aware of and am confident that these findings cannot be disputed. In the course of meditation on the esoteric, historical, mythological and scientific material available today, I have formed my own opinion of the structure of the universe which I perceive as the truth. Silver Birch, in his own inimitable manner, has the last word:

"Truth cannot enter closed minds. Truth can only find lodgement only when there is an ability to receive it. Truth, like the Great Spirit, is infinite. The amount you receive depends on your capacity. If you increase your capacity, you can receive more truth. You can never reach the stage that you know everything about the universe in which you dwell."